Revelation
and the End Times

Revelation and the End Times

Unraveling God's Message of Hope

Ben Witherington III

Abingdon Press
Nashville

REVELATION AND THE END TIMES
UNRAVELING GOD'S MESSAGE OF HOPE

Copyright © 2010 by Abingdon Press

This book is printed on acid-free paper.

Library of Congress Cataloging-in-Publication Data

Witherington, Ben, 1951-
 Revelation and the end times : unraveling God's message of hope / Ben Witherington III.
  p.   cm.
 Includes bibliographical references (p.   ).
 ISBN 978-0-687-66006-3 (book - pbk./trade pbk. : alk. paper) 1. Bible. N.T. Prophecies—End of the world. 2. End of the world—Biblical teaching. I. Title.
 BS649.E63W58 2010
 236'.9—dc22

                                                                                                2010030071

All scripture quotations unless noted otherwise are the author's translation.

10 11 12 13 14 15 16 17 18 19—10 9 8 7 6 5 4 3 2 1

MANUFACTURED IN THE UNITED STATES OF AMERICA

CONTENTS

FOREWORD

Discussions of "the end times" are nothing if not controversial, and they hardly ever produce a shrug of the shoulders. Most of us have an inherent curiosity about what will happen in the future. Furthermore, when you are a Christian and believe God has made promises and inspired prophecies about the future, curiosity is a natural response. Unfortunately, however, due to some pundits, preachers, and false prophets, the whole subject of the end times has left a bad taste in the mouths of many people. Who wants to be told that if you don't agree with this or that preacher about the future, you are headed straight to Hades; do not pass Go and do not collect your Eternal Reward?

What I hope to do in this study is examine what the New Testament actually says about the future. We will be dealing with a whole series of topics, such as: the return of Christ, the rapture, the millennium, the resurrection of believers, final judgment, heaven, hell, the "new heaven and the new earth," the devil and demons, the future of Israel, the kingdom, and the church. While not all questions about these subjects will be answered or addressed, we will work our way through a sampling of the crucial issues and subjects.

But before we even do that, let me say just briefly here that this subject is not of mere academic or historical interest. It should be of personal interest to any Christian, not just because the Bible tells us that God has a plan for our final future, but because, as Adoniram Judson, the great missionary to Burma, once said, "the future is as bright as the promises of God."

Here I want to address one preliminary issue that will move our discussion down the proper road. I remember just before the turn of the millennium I was watching a TV preacher who was arguing that Jesus would come back in the year 2000, exactly two millennia after he was born. Of course the problem was that he was saying this in 1999 and Jesus was born somewhere between 6 and 2 B.C.! So Jesus should have shown up before that preacher appeared on that program, but I guess he didn't get the memo. Such exact calculations of the return of Christ have been endless in Christian history, and thus far they have all had one thing in common—a 100 percent failure rate! But rather than just throw up our hands and say, "It's pointless to talk about it," I think we must take another tack, because when it comes to the end times we are talking not merely about our future, but about our past and present as well.

Sometimes I get asked the question: When will the end times begin? My answer to that question is quite straightforward, and it is the one the New Testament writers all would have given: *The end times began at the resurrection of Jesus.* That was the first great eschatological event, and it was followed not long thereafter by others, for instance, the falling of the Holy Spirit on Jesus' disciples, the evangelization of the whole Mediterranean crescent, and the destruction of the temple in Jerusalem in A.D. 70. In short, *the church has been in the end times for more than two thousand years*. All of church history is eschatological in that sense. *But asking about when the end times will climax or end is another question*. And it is one we will address in the pages that follow. My one request of you, my readers, is that you be patient and work all the way through this study to wait and see how I put the pieces of the puzzle together. I think in the end you will find that many of your major questions can be answered, and that it is indeed true that the future is as bright as the promises of God. There is hope for a troubled world in the eschatological material in the New Testament. You will also discover that God has revealed enough about our future to give us hope, but not so much that we don't have to live by faith. The Bible encourages great expectations—but not calculations, which lead to prognostications.

I must thank here several of my other publishers for giving me kind permission to present in this study, in a simplified form, material that appeared earlier in more detailed and technical discussions. Special thanks, then, to Eerdmans, Baylor Press, and InterVarsity for letting me edit and excerpt some material that appeared in my commentary on Romans (with Darlene Hyatt, *Paul's Letter to the Romans: A Socio-Rhetorical Commentary*, Eerdmans); in my book *The Problem with Evangelical Theology: Testing the Exegetical Foundations of Calvinism, Dispensationalism, and Wesleyanism* (Baylor); and in my eschatology study from many years ago titled *Jesus, Paul and the End of the World: A Comparative Study in New Testament Eschatology* (InterVarsity). If you are hungry for more discussion, you might peruse those sources, especially if you want additional references.

Advent 2009

CHAPTER 1

THE CHARACTER OF BIBLICAL PROPHECY

Ideas have consequences. . . . At worst, such belief [in a rapture] is a form of escapism. The hope of impending departure can lead believers to abandon interest in the world and its problems. The expectation of deteriorating conditions prior to the soon-approaching rapture is morally corrosive, encouraging pessimism, fatalism, and the forsaking of political responsibility. Disengagement from the problems of the world is ethically indefensible, but it is all too common among today's prophecy elite. Their books tell us that nuclear war is inevitable, that the pursuit of peace is pointless, that the planet's environmental woes are unstoppable, and so on. —Craig Hill, In God's Time

A. THE NATURE OF PROPHECY

A particular way of thinking called dispensationalism arose in the nineteenth century, in part due to a concern about apparently unfulfilled biblical prophecies. To their credit, dispensationalists recognized rightly that the New Testament has a profound orientation toward the end times and much to say about the future. Indeed, it even has a good deal of Old Testament prophecy that seems to have not yet been fulfilled. The problem in part with dispensationalism was not only that it did not recognize that a good deal of biblical prophecy actually *has* been fulfilled (though sometimes in a less than absolutely literal manner), but also that it did not recognize that a good deal of biblical prophecy was conditional in nature to begin with. Thus, when the conditions weren't met, the fulfillment never came.

When a prophecy began, "If my people who are called by my name will repent and turn to me," and then went on to make predictions or promises, sometimes God's people did not repent, so, therefore, prophecy did not come about. And if the people did not repent, sometimes God's mercy prevailed. Lurking behind the dispensationalist approach was the worry that unfulfilled prophecy might be seen as false prophecy, or, worse, unfulfilled prophecy might make God appear to not be a keeper of his word. Unfortunately these sorts of anxieties were answered by coming up with a view of prophecy and its character that largely ignored the original historical context and the nature of the prophecy more generally. So let us consider the matter directly.

"In the beginning was the Word" is a familiar and seemingly simple assertion; and yet its complexity, especially in an oral cultural environment, cannot be overlooked. In an ancient culture the living Word, the living voice, always had a certain weight over a written word. And of all the wordsmiths of antiquity, none had more power or authority than those who could speak for God or, in a pagan culture, for the gods. Indeed, those who could offer a divine word might well have been the most important persons.

It is not at all surprising that a study of prophecy in antiquity reveals that apparently almost all such cultures had some persons who exercised roles we would call prophetic. I have written a detailed study of prophecy elsewhere but will here summarize some of the salient points.[1] Prophecy did not begin with the period of the Israelite monarchy, nor did it end when that monarchy was eclipsed, for even in Israel prophecy in some forms carried on beyond that period of time. Nor were the prophets of Israel, any more than the New Testament prophets, operating in a cultural vacuum. It was possible for a Balaam or a Jonah or a Paul to cross cultural boundaries and still be recognized as some sort of prophetic figure. This is because the social functions and roles, and to some degree even the forms and contents of the messages, were the same in the eastern part of the Mediterranean.

Whether we are talking about the period of the Babylonian Empire or the Roman Empire, there were certain traits that marked out prophetic figures, such that they could be recognized throughout the region as some sort of spokesman or spokeswoman for the divine and could cross cultural and ethnic boundaries and still function. Indeed, prophecy was such a cross-cultural phenomenon that Babylonian kings might well have Jewish prophets serving in their courts, and Roman emperors might well listen to the word of a Jewish prophet before making a major decision. If one wants to understand biblical prophecy, one necessarily must be prepared to fish with a large net.

It is worth pondering why it is such a large proportion of the Hebrew Scriptures involves prophetic books, while the New Testament, unless one counts Revelation, contains no books that could be called prophetic as a whole or even any that, in the main, involve collections of oracles. *Could it be because the New Testament writers believed that they already lived in an age when these prophecies, through and as a result of the Christ event, were rapidly being fulfilled?* Yes, this is indeed part of the truth, but there are also many clues about Hebrew prophecy being a part of the larger ancient Near Eastern phenomenon that were missed.

While there was a range of things that prophets might do and say in the ancient world, nonetheless their activities, the forms of their discourse, and the social purposes and effects of this discourse were similar in all Mediterranean cultures, so much so that a person traveling from, say, Rome to the extremes of the eastern end of the empire in the first century A.D. could speak about prophets and prophecy and expect most any audience to have a reasonably clear notion of the subject matter. Similarly, during the time of Jeremiah one could travel from Babylon to Jerusalem and expect the social phenomenon of prophecy to be in many, though not all, ways the same in a variety of these cultures. The story of Jonah, like the story of Balaam, encourages us to look at prophecy as a cross-cultural phenomenon, with influence moving in various directions through the course of time.

I have discovered in my odyssey through the prophetic material that a great deal of loose talk has been allowed to pass for critical thinking about who prophets were and what the nature of their utterances was. For example, in the field of biblical studies, prophecy is often simply lumped together with preaching or with the creative handling and interpreting of earlier sacred texts. Part of this lack of clarity may be put down to confusion about the difference between prophetic utterances and the resulting books of prophetic material, collected and edited by scribes over time. *We need to distinguish between the prophetic experience, the prophetic expression, the prophetic tradition, and the prophetic body of literature.*

I have been struck again and again by how, across a variety of cultural lines and over the course of an enormous amount of time, Jews, pagans, and Christians who lived in the eastern end of the Mediterranean Crescent all seemed to have reasonably clear and reasonably similar ideas about what constituted a prophet and prophecy. For example, *a prophet was an oracle, a mouthpiece for some divine being, and as such he or she did not speak for himself or herself but for another.* A prophet might also be many other things (teacher, priest, sage), but the role of prophet was distinct from all others.

Prophecy, whether from Mari, Jerusalem, Delphi, or Rome, was spoken in known languages, usually in poetic form, and so was an intelligible, even if often puzzling, kind of communication. It might involve spontaneous utterances or a reading of omens or signs of various sorts, but in any case it was *not* a matter of deciphering ancient texts, which was the task of scribes and sages of various sorts. Furthermore, consulting a prophet was an attempt to obtain a current word from one or another deity about something pressing or impending. In sociological terms the prophet was seen as someone who mediated between the human and divine worlds, which, therefore, made the prophet very important but also subjected him or her to being pushed to the margins of society if the divine words involved curses rather than blessings, judgment rather than redemption.

At least in the setting of Israel and early Christianity, the prophet was one who deliberately stood at the boundary of the community—the boundary between God and the community, but also the boundary between the community and those outside it. It was the task of the prophet to call God's people to account and to reinforce the prescribed boundaries of the community while reestablishing or reinforcing the divine-human relationship. Prophets served as God's prosecuting attorney for the covenant lawsuit when Israel broke the covenant.

This takes us to another factor, which has too often been underplayed, perhaps in order to avoid the embarrassment of having to say that a particular favorite prophet might be wrong. I am referring to the fact that prophecy was, more often than not, predictive in character, though most often its subject matter dealt with something thought to be on the *near* horizon, not something decades, much less centuries, in the future. And even when the more remote future was the subject of prophecy, the subject was raised because it was thought to have a direct bearing on the present. In short, ancient prophets and prophetesses were not armchair speculators about remote subjects. Nostradamus would not have felt comfortable in this company, nor would the interpreters of the Mayan calendar, which allegedly targets 2012 as the date for the end of the world!

As a close reading of Isaiah 40–66 shows, biblical prophecy about the more distant horizon was deliberately less specific and more universal in character, dealing with not only ideas and themes the immediate audience could understand, but also themes that could transcend the immediate and particular circumstances of those listening to the prophet. Almost all oracles have something of a poetic form, but prophecy about the more remote future tends to involve even more metaphor, simile, and poetic devices, for example, hyperbole, to make the point.

Thus when prophets talk about Eden renewed with lions lying down with lambs and swords being beaten into plowshares, not only are such images *not* code words for modern concerns like the cessation of nuclear weapon stockpiling, but also they are *not* about building factories in antiquity where swords would literally be beaten into plowshares. Metaphors like these are, rather, ways of speaking about putting a stop to hostilities. It is especially interesting that when the Old Testament prophets, including Ezekiel, Daniel, and Zechariah, thought about the more distant future, they did not dwell on impending doom or Armageddon, but rather on eventual redemption and restoration of God's people and the return to Eden-like conditions.

These predictions were indeed meant to be taken *seriously* as they referred to real events, but the prophets used figures of speech that were not intended to be taken *literally*. Taking these figures of speech literally does the Bible a great disservice, and it violates the character of biblical prophecy many times over. There is in addition the problem of mistaking material that was fulfilled long ago in Israel or fulfilled in a more general way in biblical times as material awaiting a literal fulfillment as the Christian era nears an end. However, Jesus was not joking when he said that the events leading up to the destruction of the temple in Jerusalem would all occur within a generation (see Mark 13). This did happen! Only a minority of what is said in Matthew 24–25 or Mark 13 has any bearing on current or future events as we view them in the beginning of the twenty-first century, precisely because they already happened in the debacles leading up to and including the Jewish war with Rome in A.D. 70 when the temple and all Jerusalem were utterly destroyed.

B. THE NATURE OF THE APOCALYPTIC

The way apocalyptic literature is often treated by those on the far right and the far left of the theological spectrum is problematic. On the one hand, some treat it as a hard-and-fast prescription for the future, while, on the other hand, others treat it as some sort of imaginative fiction. However, when I refer to apocalyptic literature, I am referring to those biblical texts that refer to the end times—Daniel, Ezekiel, Zechariah, and Revelation. But what is apocalyptic literature? Here is a definition that begins to help us decipher such material followed by an orienting discussion.

The Society of Biblical Literature definition, arising out of its seminar on apocalyptic literature, is a good starting point. It says that an apocalypse is "a genre of revelatory literature with a narrative framework, in which a revelation is mediated by an otherworldly being to a human recipient, disclosing a transcendent reality which is both temporal, insofar as it envisages eschatological salvation, and spatial insofar as it involves another, supernatural world."[2] To this definition is sometimes added the statement that this literature is minority literature written in coded language to comfort a group of believers undergoing some sort of crisis.

The essence of the definition is that present, mundane reality is interpreted in light of both the supernatural world and the future. For the book of Revelation, for example, this entails beginning with the present experiences of the churches and trying to help them interpret and endure those experiences in the light of the larger perspective that John's visions of what is above and beyond give them. This particular book is clearly minority literature written in a somewhat coded way for persons enduring crisis.

Eschatological concepts, or ideas related to end times, are not necessarily the heart of what the apocalyptic is all about, for they are found in many types of early Jewish and Christian literature. For that matter there are apocalypses that do not really focus on what final form the future will take. Apocalyptic, then, is primarily a matter of the use of a *distinctive form*—visions with often bizarre and hyperbolic (extreme, larger than life) metaphors and images. Some apocalypses focus almost entirely on otherworldly journeys without saying much about the end of human history. In other words, historical apocalypses are not the only kind of apocalypse.

The very heart of apocalyptic is the unveiling of secrets and truths about God's perspective on a variety of thorny subjects including justice, the problem of evil, and what God proposes to do about such matters. This literature was the dominant form of prophecy in Jewish contexts from the second century B.C. to the second century A.D., and it reflects the fact that its authors believed they lived in the age when earlier prophecies were being fulfilled, and, therefore, it was right to contemplate what God's final answer and solution would be. This dominance of apocalyptic literature also reflects the deeply held conviction that God's people lived in dark times when God's hand in matters and God's will for believers were not clear. Indeed, in some ways it *was* a secret or a mystery. God's plan had to be revealed to us, because it was not self-evident.

A major shift occurred from traditional prophecy, speaking for God about the present or future, to apocalyptic prophecy, speaking primarily about the end times. The difference was not because there were no prophets around (for example, John the Baptist), but because of the conviction that God's people were living at the dawn of or actually in the end times. The final things had already been set in motion, and under such circumstances it was necessary to talk about them.

C. AND SO?

It is no accident that the historical apocalypses began to disappear from Jewish literature after A.D. 70 and from Christian literature in the second and third centuries A.D. Otherworldly journeys, however, such as what we find in John's Revelation or even, much later, in Dante's *Divine Comedy*, continue to be produced. In fact, references to otherworldly eschatology and mysticism increased the closer one got to the Middle Ages. The grip of eschatology on believers that took the form of "the end is now" gradually loosened after the first century A.D. This is as true of Jewish as of Christian literature. A futurist eschatological outlook explains much about Jesus and the earliest Christian belief system, as well as the belief system of the author of Revelation.[3]

What is completely lost in the shuffle in much of the popular discussion of such material is not merely literary sensitivity to the sort of material one is dealing with, but the recognition that these prophecies were the word of God for Jews and Christians many centuries ago and that they also had meaning for those audiences. Indeed, they were written for those audiences in the first place, not for us. *What the text meant then is still what the text means today. And what it could not possibly have meant in the first century A.D. or before, it does not mean now.* These texts were not written to scare the living daylights out of us. The Christian authors of the oracles in the New Testament believed that their own immediate audiences already lived in the age of fulfillment, already lived in the end times.

One of the major points I have made in my earlier study of prophecy is that it is important to distinguish between prophetic experience, prophetic expression, and the prophetic tradition. The book of Revelation is certainly not simply a transcript of a prophetic experience. Rather, in his book the seer has incorporated into a complex whole a report of his vision or visions that he reflects upon *in light of the Hebrew Scriptures and a variety of other sources*. In other words, John had visions, and then fashioned them as an apocalyptic prophetic work to express not merely what he had seen, but what bearing that vision had on his audiences. This means we might well not have an apocalypse *at all* if John had not been exiled at some distance from his audiences.

But we should not imagine John, the author of Revelation, on Patmos poring over Hebrew Scripture scrolls and then creating a literary patchwork quilt. The visions that came to John came not only to a Scripture-saturated mind, but also to a mind well acquainted with popular and mythical images of his larger Greco-Roman world. What John heard, he may well have transcribed almost verbatim; but what he saw, he had to describe. Thus he drew on his existing mental resources. When anyone sees images and symbols in odd combination, one must grope for analogies to describe the experience (hence John's repeated use of the phrase "it was like…"). One must resort to metaphorical, mythological, and sometimes multivalent language. By "multivalent" I mean language that has multiple possible meanings, because it is a sort of universal symbolic language. The fact that these symbols are broadly understood helps explain why works such as Revelation have been able to communicate across time and why these works were seen as important and preserved. But paradoxically, it is also true that apocalyptic prophecy always requires interpretation or explanation. It is indeed a sort of coded language, and those not aware of the meaning will be in the dark unless they receive some help.

While it is certainly true that there are various examples of otherworldly visions in Revelation, it is crucial to bear in mind that this work is not just about what is transpiring in heaven. The seer is not simply a mystic. There is also a historical *and* an eschatological dimension to this book, not only in the opening letters but also in the descriptions of destruction followed by a new earth as well as a new heaven. John is concerned, not just about a heaven that is spatially near, but about events that are thought to be temporally near. His focus is not just *up* there, but also *out* there. While it is a product of our modern tendency to separate the social and the spiritual, or the mundane and the supernatural, one might find the notion of traffic between heaven and earth, or of an open heaven and an influenced earth, or indeed of a merger between heaven and earth (Rev. 21–22), somewhat off-putting. John has not substituted an otherworldly view of eternity for an earlier more temporal, historical, eschatological one. Rather, the two are intertwined here. On the other hand, it also will not do to assume that John himself believed he was simply using mythical images to describe all-too-mundane realities. John really believed not merely in God and the Christ and angels but in their regular interaction with humankind in the earthly sphere. The angels, for instance, are not symbols or figures of human beings. One should not be misled by the hyperbolic nature and rhetorical dimensions of some of the images into thinking that this material is not intended to refer to something concrete. It is, but the references are sometimes to human figures and sometimes to superhuman ones.

CHAPTER 2

THE RETURN OF THE KING

God will invade. But I wonder whether people who ask
God to interfere openly and directly in our world quite realize what it will be like when He does. When that happens,
it is the end of the world. When the author walks on to the
stage the play is over. God is going to invade, all right: but
what is the good of saying you are on His side then, when
you see the whole natural universe melting away like a
dream and something else—something it never entered your
head to conceive—comes crashing in; something so beautiful to some of us and so terrible to others that none of us will
have any choice left? For this time it will be God without
disguise; something so overwhelming that it will strike either
irresistible love or irresistible horror into every creature. It
will be too late then to choose your side. There is no use
saying you choose to lie down when it has become impossible to stand up. —C. S. Lewis, Mere Christianity

"Many happy returns!" said the lady at the checkout counter as I was doing my Christmas shopping. I suppose she was trying to be clever, especially during the Advent season, but of course she was just talking about my purchases. I, on the other hand, was thinking about the first Sunday of Advent where we celebrate, not the first coming of Christ, but rather his return. This is why on that Sunday in the church calendar we sing the hymn Charles Wesley altered and reworked—"Lo, He Comes with Clouds Descending." At the first coming, Jesus did not make a grand entrance trailing clouds of glory. But at the second coming, as C. S. Lewis puts it, it will be God on earth without disguise—something totally overwhelming.

The Scriptures say that for God one day is as a thousand years and a thousand years is as one day, but for us two thousand years and counting is a very long time indeed. It is so long, in fact, that many, both outside and within the church, have been led to ask impatiently, "Where is the promise of his coming?" or "How long, O Lord?" Even some of the devout have had their fervor run cold when it comes to the return of Christ. They are so leery and weary of poor soothsayers that they have practically, if not cognitively and officially, given up hope of the return of Christ and resigned themselves to life here, death hereafter, and hopefully heaven thereafter. This is a tragedy because it leads to giving up on this world's future and accepts, in exchange, a pleasant future for at least some of us in another world. This, however, must be called Esau's bargain. Like Esau in Genesis 25:29-34—selling one's birthright for something that brings some personal satisfaction but at the end of the day is less than what the New Testament promises: our "new birth" right. What, then, does the New Testament promise when it comes to the return of the King? In order to understand how the New Testament writers envision this happening, we need to understand how a mundane human king returns to his city.

A. A ROYAL VISITATION AND A ROYAL WELCOME

Tucked away in the second half of Psalm 24 is an entrance liturgy. It reads:

Lift up your heads, O gates,
   And be lifted up, O ancient doors,
   That the King of glory may come in!
Who is the King of glory?
   The Lord strong and mighty,
   The Lord mighty in battle.
Lift up your heads, O gates,
   And lift them up, O ancient doors,
   That the King of glory may come in!
Who is this King of glory?
   The Lord of hosts,
   He is the King of glory. (vv. 7-10)

What is envisioned here was a rather common scene. A king has been away, perhaps away in a far country fighting battles. He, his entourage, and his army return to his own capital city. Like most ancient cities it is a walled city, and perched on the wall is a watchman scanning the horizon. The watchman sees the cloud of dust kicked up by a coming multitude, led by a herald with a trumpet. It is the herald who goes out in front of the royal party, blows his trumpet, and then gives a cry of command for the gates to be opened—the doors to be flung back so that the king can enter. The watchman, rightly enough, responds to the herald by saying the ancient equivalent of "Stand and identify." The herald then identifies the royal figure (in this case the King of glory, the Lord mighty in battle).

The entrance liturgy in Psalm 24 ends at this juncture, but those who knew the protocols knew what came next. Once the watchman on the wall was satisfied with the identification, the gates would be opened, and then a greeting committee would go out to meet the king and his party on the road in front of the city. They would welcome him home and then escort him back into the city with much fanfare. There would be a royal processional into the city with much pomp and circumstance and cries of celebration. You can get something of the sense of this by simply rereading the story of Jesus' triumphal entry into Jerusalem in Mark 11:1-11. It was a time of joy and celebration. The king had returned home alive and well, and all manner of things would now be well for all. It is precisely this scenario and this imagery that are used in the New Testament to describe what is called variously the parousia, the appearing of Christ, or the second coming.

What, exactly, is the parousia? And why was this term chosen to refer to the return of Christ? What difference, if any, does it make if we use the literal meaning of this word? As it turns out, it makes a considerable difference to the interpretation of this event.

It has been argued, for instance, that *parousia* refers merely to "presence" in 1 Thessalonians and that what is envisioned is not a descent but rather an unveiling, with a removal of the barrier between earth and heaven, like the raising of a curtain. The Greek text of 1 Thessalonians 4:16, however, speaks of Jesus coming down from heaven. As for the meaning of *parousia*, Paul *can* use the term to mean "presence" (2 Cor. 10:10; Phil. 2:12) in a noneschatological context, but he also uses it to mean "coming" in a noneschatological context (1 Cor. 16:17; 2 Cor. 7:6-7). The question is, how is Paul using it in a context like this one in 1 Thessalonians 4 that describes the end times?

We must bear in mind that already in the Hellenistic period (323–146 B.C.), the word had come to have a special association with the arrival of significant persons; and when coupled with the language of coming down, the word *parousia* is unlikely to mean anything else here. In fact, most commentators say, looking at the majority of evidence, that every time this word appears in an eschatological context it means "coming" or "arrival." The word in its primary sense has a sense of movement. A good example of the usage in a Hellenistic context in connection with an arrival and a greeting of a royal figure can be found in Josephus,[1] *Ant.* 11.26–28, where a priest is awaiting the parousia of Alexander in order to go out and meet him.

Everywhere else in the New Testament the term is used in the eschatological sense of the coming or arrival of the Lord or Son of Man (Matt. 24:27-39; James 5:7; 2 Pet. 1:16; 3:4; 1 John 2:28). Ernest Best concludes, "The secular significance of *parousia* reinforces the conception of a coming of Christ which is a public event, in which he returns from 'outside' history to end history and which therefore eliminates any idea of a gradual development of events within history which themselves share the End."[2]

Last, it seems clear that the concept enshrined in this term is found in the Aramaic prayer *marana tha*, "Come, O Lord" (1 Cor. 16:22). We must conclude that the translation "presence" in 1 Thessalonians 4–5 or elsewhere suits neither the eschatological context nor the history of the use of the term when speaking of "lords" or royal figures, and Paul always uses the term *parousia* in 1 Thessalonians in connection with the term *lord* (2:19; 3:13; 4:15; 5:23).

The difference, of course, was that Christ is envisioned as returning from heaven, trailing clouds of glory, not kicking up clouds of dust on a war charger. But still the imagery used is that of a returning triumphant king, adopted and adapted to the circumstances New Testament writers believed would occur when Christ returned. Here is how Paul describes that great and fearsome Day of the Lord in 1 Thessalonians 4:13-18:

> Brothers and sisters, we do not want you to be ignorant about those who fall asleep, or to grieve like the rest of human beings, who have no hope. We believe that Jesus died and rose again and so we believe that God will bring with Jesus those

who have fallen asleep in him. According to the Lord's own word, we tell you that we who are still alive, who are left till the coming of the Lord, will certainly not precede those who have fallen asleep. For the Lord himself will come down from heaven, with a loud command, with the voice of the archangel and with the trumpet call of God, and the dead in Christ will rise first. After that, we who are still alive and are left will be caught up together with them in the clouds to meet the Lord in the air. And so we will be with the Lord forever. Therefore encourage each other with these words.

First of all, notice what Paul says about the Lord coming down from heaven with a loud cry of command—in the entrance liturgy this would be the cry for the gates to open. In this version of the entrance liturgy, it is the cry for the gates of the land of the dead to open and the command for the dead in Christ to arise and come forth to the Lord. Second, there is clarification that the person doing the heralding is, in fact, the archangel who descends with Christ blowing a trumpet loud enough to wake the dead! Hark, the herald angels, indeed! Thus in this scenario, first the dead in Christ will arise, then those Christians alive at the time will rise up to meet Christ in the air with the departed saints. This is the traditional greeting committee going out to welcome the king back into his realm or dominion. Everyone listening to these words would know what comes next—the King with the greeting party descends back to the earthly realm, where they will be together evermore and Christ will reign on the earth forever. Paul ends by saying that the Thessalonians, currently persecuted and facing difficult times, should encourage one another with this promise of the return of the King.

During the last almost two hundred years of church history, a very different interpretation of this text has arisen in some conservative Protestant circles called dispensationalism. These people say that this text is the "rapture" of the church out of the world before or during the final period of great tribulation upon the earth. So far as I can tell, this interpretation of 1 Thessalonians 4 did not exist before about 1820, when the notion of rapture was first offered. This interpretation has become enormously popular, particularly in North America, and has been the basis of all kinds of endless speculation about the timing and character of the return of Christ. Would there be two second comings—one invisible and one visible? Would Jesus come for the church first and then to judge the world? The problems with this sort of speculation are manifold.

First of all there is the problem that, while Paul is certainly talking about meeting the Lord in the air, "the air" is not heaven in Paul's cosmology or worldview. It is simply the earth's atmosphere, and nothing is said about going from the earth's atmosphere to heaven in this passage. Second, the Thessalonians would have recognized the echoes of the royal entrance liturgy in the terminology Paul used here, especially with the reference to the trumpet, the cry of command, and the herald going before the King. They would assume that what came next, after greeting Christ in the air, was a return to earth with the King where he would rule his domain, for "the earth is the Lord's and the fullness thereof" (Ps. 24:1). Consider the interpretation of this very text by one of the earliest and most astute students of Paul, John Chrysostom, who says:

> For when a king drives into a city, those who are honorable go out to meet him; but the condemned await the judge within. And upon the coming of an affectionate father, his children indeed, and those who are worthy to be his children, are taken out in a chariot, that they may see him and kiss him; but the housekeepers who have offended him remain within. (*Hom. 1 Thess.* 8)

In the book of Thessalonians, Paul is dealing with a pastoral problem. There are Christians who have died in Thessalonike, and those left living are worried that their dead fellow believers may be left out of the resurrection from the dead when Christ comes, since they died before that event. Paul is not offering some sort of escape plan for the living who suffer during the final tribulation on earth, he is reassuring the audience that beyond death there will be a victory, a resurrection of the dead.

When you think about it, why should the last generation of Christians be exempt from suffering or martyrdom when no previous generation of the faithful have been? And how would a message about this much later exemption comfort the first-century Thessalonians about their beloved deceased family members and friends who had not been exempt from giving the last full measure for their faith in Christ? This whole line of thinking does not take into account the original context of

1 Thessalonians. But what about those other so-called rapture texts in the New Testament? We will deal with them at some length later in this study.

Concentrating now on what 1 Thessalonians 4:13-18 *is* actually discussing, Paul uses a phrase that has caused some confusion: "we who remain, who are left when the Lord returns." Some scholars have long thought this was clear evidence that Paul believed Jesus would return in his lifetime. However, this overlooks several important points: (1) Paul elsewhere uses the controlling metaphor of the thief coming in the night to describe how and when Christ will return—at an unexpected time he will break into our midst suddenly (see 1 Thess. 5:2, a metaphor he got from the teachings of Jesus [see Luke 12:38-40; 17:34]); (2) Paul had to conjure with two unknowns—the timing of his own death and the timing of the return of Christ. Since he did not know the timing of either and considered it possible that Christ *might* return during his lifetime, he could not have said "but we who are dead when the Lord returns...." To say that would have implied he had definite knowledge about the timing of either of these events, which, in fact, he did not. Hence 1 Thessalonians 4:13-18 does not suggest that Paul was convinced Christ *must* return during his lifetime, and, therefore, there is no reason to conclude that he wrongly calculated that date. The date was unknown. In fact, it was unknown even to Jesus himself.

The material in 1 Thessalonians 4 does not stand alone. Indeed, it leads immediately into a continued discussion of the same matter in 1 Thessalonians 5. There we are told very clearly that Paul has no need to tell the people of Thessalonica again, though he will do so, that Christ will come like a thief in the night. The difference between the situation of the believers and unbelievers when Christ comes is not that the former group knows the timing of the second coming and the latter does not. The difference is that believers know Christ will definitely return at some juncture, and so they should no more be surprised by that event than one is surprised that sunrise eventually follows night, however long the darkness may last.

B. TIMING IS *NOT* EVERYTHING

Mark 13:32 is Jesus' clearest statement about the timing of his return. What he says is that no human being, no angel, and not even the Son knows the timing of that day. The phrase "the day and the hour no one knows" means that not merely the precise time, but the timing in general, is unknown. This verse should have put an end to Christian theological weather forecasting, but sadly it hasn't. Let me be as clear as I can: *There is no encouragement in the New Testament itself to speculate about the timing of the return of Christ. What is said about the matter is that it will come at an unexpected time, and come suddenly. No one knows when Christ will return. Therefore, the church must always be ready, always be the church expectant.*

Let us turn briefly to other texts that seem to comment on the timing of Christ's return. Let us consider two that come right at the end of the Bible in Revelation 22:12, 20—two verses that should be compared to Revelation 1:1. The Greek here in the latter case involves the phrase *en taxei* (Rev. 1:1) and the former two texts simply use the word *taxu* (Rev. 22:12, 20). The key word is the word that is transliterated into English as *taxi!* Yes, taxi. What it means is "quick" or, as an adverb, "quickly." When the word modifies a verb such as "coming," it ought to be translated as an adverb—quickly. For example, "Behold, I am coming quickly." The translation of Revelation 1:1 should read "what must happen in a hurry, or with dispatch, or quickly." In other words, these texts are not making comments on *when* Jesus is coming but on *how*—quickly, suddenly. This comports nicely with the thief in the night metaphor. The same can be said about Revelation 22:12, 20—the prayer is for Jesus to come quickly, whether it is sooner or later. But let us consider another text sometimes thought to predict something about the timing of Christ's return.

Philippians 4:4-5 says, "Rejoice in the Lord always. Again I say, rejoice.... The Lord is near [or at hand]." Here one needs to know the Old Testament texts Paul has in mind when he offers these imperatives. He likely has in mind Psalm 145:18: "The Lord is near to those who call upon him," or possibly Psalm 34:18: "The Lord is near to the brokenhearted." In both these texts the word *near* refers to spatial nearness, not nearness in time; and in view of the context in Philippians 4, it is likely the word has the same nuance here. But what about a verse like Mark 9:1?

In Mark 9:1 Jesus tells his disciples, "Truly I tell you that there are some standing here who will not taste death until they see the kingdom of God has come in power." The first point to note about this verse is that the subject is not Jesus, but rather the kingdom of God; and as for that kingdom, Jesus had already said numerous times that it was breaking into the midst of his audience *during* his ministry. But what did he mean by saying that some standing with him would see it come with power before they died? There are, in fact, three possible referents here: (1) the transfiguration of Jesus; (2) the resurrection of Jesus; (3) the pouring out of the Spirit on the disciples at Pentecost. In all three cases we are talking about eschatological events that could be seen as examples of the kingdom coming in power on earth. What has confused some is the proximity of Mark 9:1 to Mark 8:38, which probably is about the second coming of Christ. Here we read: "when he comes in the glory of his Father with his holy messengers/angels"; however, if "messengers" is the right translation, then Mark 8:38 could refer to the transfiguration when Christ was glorified and Elijah and Moses seemed to show up. In any case, the Son of Man is not the same as the kingdom, and vice versa. In its context the most likely referent for Mark 9:1 *is* the story of the transfiguration, which follows immediately in Mark 9:2-8 and chronologically happens only about a week later. Notice as well that Mark 9:1 says only "some of you." It does not say that "all of you" will see this and, as you may recall, only three disciples were privileged to witness the transfiguration.

We could continue to go down this road, but the conclusion would still be the same: *On close examination, there are no errant predictions in the New Testament saying that Christ would return during the lifetime of those Christians who lived in the first century* A.D. While it was considered *possible* that such a return could happen in that era, none of the New Testament writers made the mistake of speculating about the precise timing of Christ's return. The early Christians had great hopes and expectations, but did not give way to calculations and predictions. So what is the difference?

Expectations leave the outcome and the timing of events where such matters should be left—in the hands of God. Calculations and prognostications, however, amount to a failure of trust and faith, a failure of nerve and heart. Calculations are the all-too-human attempt to control the future, to get a clear fix on its outcome, to try to know more than even Jesus knew when he said, "Of that day or hour, no one knows." Prognostications amount to a failure to trust God about the future. Prognosticating involves a presumption to know some things that none of us know and an unwillingness to simply trust that God has things in hand. God has revealed enough about the future to give us hope, but not so much that we do not have to live by faith every day for the rest of our lives.

Consider the possible negative consequences for us if we knew exactly when Christ would return. First, we could assume that we had plenty of time to do what we wanted, plenty of time to repent later for our sins, plenty of time to sow our wild oats, since Jesus isn't coming back in the next _____ (fill in the blank) months or years. Second, we would place our trust not in God but in what we believe we know about the timing of Christ's return, in short in our own knowledge and ability to know and properly interpret the future. This way leads to both pride and madness. Third, it has in fact led some persons in the modern era to say, "Well, those early Christians did not know as much about the end times as we know now. For instance, they did not understand the book of Revelation as well as do we who are living these events now." Do you hear the hubris and exaggerated self-importance in that argument? I would say just the opposite. The original Christians who lived in the era when these promises and prophecies were given were far *more* likely to understand them and interpret them rightly than we are, because they understood Jewish apocalyptic prophecy and its many symbols and ideas far better than we do now.

In our previous chapter we looked at Jewish prophecy to really get a handle on this complex material. Here it is enough to reiterate that it is the height of arrogance to say that we know better than the inspired writers of Scripture what they actually meant when they said this or that! In fact, we do not even know as much as the audiences of those inspired writers knew, especially when it comes to the more opaque and metaphorical prophecies of Scripture.

C. SNAPSHOT—WHAT HAPPENS WHEN CHRIST RETURNS

Here is the place to address the issues of the events that are said to ensue when Christ does return. The right place to start this discussion is with some selected verses in 1 Corinthians 15:

But Christ has indeed been raised from the dead, the firstfruits of those who have fallen asleep. For since death came through a man, the resurrection of the dead comes also through a man. For as in Adam all die, so in Christ all will be made alive. But each in his own turn: Christ, the firstfruits; then, when he comes, those who belong to him. Then the end will come, when he hands over the kingdom to God the Father after he has destroyed all dominion, authority and power. For he must reign until he has put all his enemies under his feet. The last enemy to be destroyed is death. For he "has put everything under his feet." Now when it says that "everything" has been put under him, it is clear that this does not include God himself, who put everything under Christ. When he has done this, then the Son himself will be made subject to him who put everything under him, so that God may be all in all. (vv. 20-28 NIV)

Let's first deal with the concept of firstfruits and latter fruits, an agricultural metaphor used by Paul to explain the relationship between Jesus' bodily resurrection and that of those who are in Christ when Christ returns. Paul does not see Christ's resurrection as an isolated and unique event in the middle of human history. He sees it as a preview of coming attractions, the foretaste of what God has in mind for the saints. What happened to Jesus is said to be exactly the same thing that will happen for Christians when he returns. *Christ's history is the believer's destiny,* according to Paul. This is perhaps why Paul speaks of Christ as the last or eschatological Adam. On this showing the risen Christ is the last founder of a whole new race of human beings, ones who are neither Jew nor Gentile but rather new creatures in Christ, awaiting their complete conformity to the image of Christ by means of bodily resurrection. We will say much more about resurrection in the New Testament in a subsequent chapter, but here we need to concentrate on the order of events that Paul outlines for us:

1. the return of Christ with his angels and saints;
2. the resurrection of dead Christians and the transformation of living Christians who go out to meet him in the air and join with him in reigning as the kingdom comes on earth, as it is in heaven;
3. the destruction of all the anti-God powers and rulers upon the earth; and
4. the demise of death, the last enemy.
5. Then Christ will subject himself once more to the Father and turn the kingdom back over to the Father.

There is material found elsewhere that could be used to expand this scenario, even in other letters of Paul. For example, Paul believes that one of the things that will happen when Christ returns is that many Jews will accept him then as their Messiah (see Rom. 11), and another is the judgment of the living and the dead even involving the judgment of Christians' own deeds (see 2 Cor. 5:10). You can see that all these end-time events and scenarios are intertwined, and it is difficult to talk about one aspect without talking about several of them at once. *What is important to say here is that the return of the King is the trigger event, which sets in motion the end of the end times, and it begins to become clear that humankind's destiny is brought to its final conclusion not in heaven, but on earth, at the end of time after the return of Christ.*

D. AND SO?

What have we learned thus far in this discussion?

1. We have learned that both the first and second comings of Christ were seen as eschatological events of vital importance to human history and especially for followers of Christ.

2. We have learned that it was the fact of Christ's return and a sure confidence it would happen, not the timing of that return, that generated the outlook of New Testament writers.

3. We have learned that there are good reasons why God did not reveal the timing of Christ's return to us; namely, so we would have to live by faith and in hope day after day, trusting not in our own reasoning or calculations but in God for the future. We may not know all that the future holds, but we do know who holds the future in his hands—our Lord and Savior Jesus.

4. But we have also learned that when Christ returns, instead of the full-stop end of all things, what will happen is the final state of affairs, on earth as it is in heaven, when the kingdoms of this world become the kingdom of our God and of his Christ. But what happens to us if we die before the return of Christ? Where do we go? We must address the issue of the other world in the next chapter.

CHAPTER 3

THE OTHER WORLD— HEAVEN AND HELL

Many people want to go to heaven the way they want to go to Florida—they think the weather will be an improvement and the people decent. But the biblical heaven is not a nice environment far removed from the stress of hard city life. It is the invasion of the city by the City. We enter heaven not by escaping what we don't like, but by the sanctification of the place in which God has placed us. There is not so much as a hint of escapism in St. John's heaven. This is not a long (eternal) weekend away from the responsibilities of employment and citizenship, but the intensification and healing of them. —Eugene Peterson, Reversed Thunder

I was doing a funeral for a man who never attended church, and it was interesting to just be a fly on the wall and listen to the conversation around the punch bowl at the reception afterward. One person said, "John was such a good man. He used to come and mow my grass when Ralph was out of town. If he doesn't get into heaven, no one will." It's actually not a very unusual comment. One Gallup poll shows that 70 percent of Americans want to go, and think they are going, to heaven, and when asked about the entrance requirements, one of the most frequent responses is "being a good person"—so much for the doctrine of salvation by grace through faith.

Unfortunately what has happened in the modern Christian discussion about the afterlife is that instead of placing the emphasis where the New Testament places it—which is on the new heaven and the new earth once Christ returns—we have focused on heaven and hell, and indeed this has been the case in Christendom ever since Dante's classic work *The Divine Comedy* came out in the Middle Ages.

It is interesting that when one surveys what the New Testament says about heaven and hell, Jesus actually has more to say about hell than heaven, although neither topic comes up very frequently. Furthermore, not too many scholars have noticed the remarkable fact that Paul says almost nothing about hell at all, even though we have more of his writings in the New Testament than of any other single author (making up more than 40 percent of the New Testament). What's up with that? Comments on such subjects are scattered, sparse, and sporadic. By contrast, comments on the second coming of Christ, the coming kingdom of God, the future of God's people, resurrection, the millennium, and the new heaven and new earth are considerably more frequent. So let's see what the New Testament actually says about heaven and hell.

A. JESUS ON HEAVEN AND HELL

Gehenna. It's an odd word; indeed, it's an Aramaic form of a name—Hinnom. It refers to a place south of the city of David, namely, the Hinnom Valley. When Jesus wants to talk about the negative place in the afterlife, he calls it Gehenna. But why? There are two possible reasons.

First, there is the history of what happened in the Hinnom Valley just on the south side of Jerusalem. Before Jesus' time it had been the site where idolatrous Jews sacrificed their children to the god Molech (2 Chron. 28:3; 33:6; Jer. 7:31; 19:2-6). It was a place of uncleanness and horror in the Jewish imagination.

But, as discovered by archaeologists, it had a more recent history. Apparently it was the garbage dump for Jerusalem in Jesus' day. This makes sense because Jesus talks about Gehenna as a place where "the worm does not die, and the fire does not go out" (Mark 9:48). The ancients burned their garbage sometimes; and, in any case, they did not separate wet from dry garbage. So a garbage dump in antiquity naturally attracted maggots, due to the rotting vegetation. It's a graphic image, and Jesus uses it to describe the eternally stinking, hot place that no one in their right mind would want to visit, much less dwell in. Dante got the picture clearly enough. Read the first volume of his *Divine Comedy* called *Inferno*. It is not a pretty picture.

Jesus uses the term *Gehenna* eleven times in the first three Gospels. When it comes to the fate of humans, Jesus says that Gehenna is a place where both body and human spirit can be destroyed (Matt. 10:28). In Mark 9:43 he says it is a place of unquenchable fire. This is probably where the "lake of fire" image in Revelation 20 comes from in what we today call hell. Matthew 23:33 is even more graphic. Some of Jesus' critics are warned that they are headed for the judgment of Gehenna. Gehenna is not just an unpleasant eternal destination. It's a place where one is judged or punished for one's sins. What is perhaps most notable about these passages is that they differ from the Old Testament concept of Sheol, which was simply the land of the dead, or Hades, the underworld in Greek thought, which is often also described as a land of the dead. Gehenna is described in terms that we would associate with the word *hell*. And this brings us to the interesting parable of the rich man and Lazarus.

Luke 16:19-31 is, without doubt, one of the most colorful of all Jesus' parables, and it deserves to be considered at some length for what it reveals about Jesus' views on the afterlife in another world. The trick is to not press it too hard on the details, since this is after all a fictional and metaphorical story. Not all the details are meant to be literally descriptive. Parables never work that way.

> There was a rich man who was dressed in purple and fine linen and lived in luxury every day. At his gate was laid a beggar named Lazarus, covered with sores and longing to eat what fell from the rich man's table. Even the dogs came and licked his sores. The time came when the beggar died and the angels carried him to Abraham's side. The rich man also died and was buried. In [Hades], where he was in torment, he looked up and

saw Abraham far away, with Lazarus by his side. So he called to him, "Father Abraham, have pity on me and send Lazarus to dip the tip of his finger in water and cool my tongue, because I am in agony in this fire." But Abraham replied, "Son, remember that in your lifetime you received your good things, while Lazarus received bad things, but now he is comforted here and you are in agony. And besides all this, between us and you a great chasm has been fixed, so that those who want to go from here to you cannot, nor can anyone cross over from there to us." He answered, "Then I beg you, father, send Lazarus to my father's house, for I have five brothers. Let him warn them, so that they will not also come to this place of torment."Abraham replied, "They have Moses and the Prophets; let them listen to them." "No, father Abraham," he said, "but if someone from the dead goes to them, they will repent." He said to him, "If they do not listen to Moses and the Prophets, they will not be convinced even if someone rises from the dead." (Luke 16:19-31 NIV)

As it happens, this story, or something very close to it, already existed in Jesus' day before he told this parable. It is not a completely new or unique creation of Jesus. Having said that, we must assume that the way Jesus adopts and adapts it for his own purposes indicates that he endorsed various of the things said in this parable about the afterlife. What, then, do we learn about Jesus' views? First, we learn that Jesus does not simply affirm the Old Testament view of the afterlife, namely the theology of Sheol. In the Old Testament when people died it was believed that they simply went to the land of the dead, called Sheol. Sometimes the phrase was used, "being gathered to his ancestors," and it hardly involves some kind of positive notion of the afterlife. The person still exists in some sort of half-life in the afterlife, which could be called neither heaven nor hell. It's just a matter of being in the land of the dead. We can see this in a text like 1 Samuel 28, where we hear about a woman who could call up the spirits of the dead and consult them, as in the case of the spirit of the prophet Samuel. Samuel in this story is viewed as still "alive," but not in heaven; rather, he is just in the land of the dead, and he is not too pleased with being bothered by this medium who summons him.

Second, by contrast with 1 Samuel 28, Jesus speaks about Father Abraham being in a positive, desirable place, a place to which angels carry devout persons, in this case a poor man named Lazarus (not the same chap as the one in John 11). This "place of Abraham" is the place that Jesus elsewhere in this same Gospel calls "Paradise," which apparently was the Jewish name for the top floor in heaven (see Luke 23:43 and compare Paul's reference to the third heaven in 2 Cor. 12:2-4).

Hades, though it is the Greek word for the underworld, here is used as a term to refer to the negative place in the otherworld, not merely the land of the dead. Here, the rich man suffers from the heat and cries out for water. This comports with what Jesus elsewhere says goes on in Gehenna, namely, the fire never is quenched. The third thing one learns about Jesus' view of the afterlife in the other world is that *this life* is the place of decision, and once you are dead it is too late to change your situation. The unalterable nature of the situation in the afterlife is further punctuated by the remark that no one can go from Abraham's side to help the man in Hades, nor is there any way to get from Hades to Paradise.

According to this parable, the choices made in this life affect, if not determine, what happens to one in the next life. It is very clear from this parable that Jesus did not agree with the Sadducees who rejected notions like resurrection or the role angels could play, perhaps particularly in the afterlife, as in this parable.

Jesus did not limit his thinking about the afterlife to what is said in the Pentateuch. His thinking is much closer to that of the Pharisees about such matters, and indeed close to what we find in the very latest parts of the Old Testament, such as in Daniel or Job where we hear a little bit about heaven and life in the other world (see Dan. 12 on resurrection). Had we just the Old Testament to go on, we might assume that your name needed to begin with E, such as Elijah or Enoch, for you to be taken up into heaven at some point during your life, because those are the persons who reportedly were taken up to God. There is not even anything said in the Old Testament about Abraham dying and going to heaven, though clearly Jesus affirms that idea in this parable.

What have we learned thus far about Jesus' views on heaven and hell?

• We have learned that Jesus believes they are real places and that one's behavior in this life affects where one goes in the next. But there is something more. We learn exactly what Jesus laments here and elsewhere—how difficult it is for a rich person to get into the kingdom of God (Mark 10:17-27). Jesus says it is as difficult as trying to squeeze a camel through the eye of a needle. His point is to suggest not that it is completely impossible, simply that it is impossible by mere human effort. Being a good person, like the rich young ruler, is not enough; rather, his riches are an encumbrance to getting to the kingdom. But what is impossible for humans is nonetheless possible for God, by grace and through faith.

• We have learned that God is a God of justice. He balances the scales. Thus this parable talks about reversal. Those who did not get their just deserts in this life will get them in the next. But by contrast those who had their cake and ate it too in this life, neglecting the poor and their responsibilities for the poor, will not be so favored in the next life. There are indeed eternal rewards for piety and purity and eternal punishments for impiety and cruelty in the next life. This may be a hard truth, but it is right there in the parable for all to see, and Jesus believed it.

If we ask the hard question of how this is reconciled with the notion of salvation by grace, the answer is as follows: Salvation is indeed a gift, but it is a gift that has to be received through faith and trusting God. The rich man in this parable showed no such faith. Our deeds or misdeeds in this life do not buy us a ticket to heaven or hell, but they do affect the rewards or punishments we receive when we get there. Like many early Jews, Jesus and Paul both talk about rewards in heaven and punishments elsewhere. Heaven itself is never the reward, but there are rewards in heaven.

Notice, for example, how in 1 Corinthians 3:10-15 Paul says that even ministers need to think seriously about how they do their ministerial works, for if they do them well, "they shall receive a reward" (v. 14), but if not, they may well be saved, but they will be escaping as through fire, by the hair on their chins! Who wants to just barely squeak by, barely getting into heaven or God's kingdom? Who wouldn't rather hear from Jesus the words "Well done, good and faithful servant. Inherit the kingdom"?

Let us turn now to that other, and final, reference to heaven in Luke's Gospel, Luke 23:39-43. This beautiful story, sometimes called the story about the penitent thief, should actually be called the story of the merciful Savior. Jesus welcomes the penitent man into Paradise; indeed, Jesus suggests the man will be in the highest part of heaven with Jesus himself! Several points are worth noting. The "thief" is actually wrongly so called, as Romans didn't crucify thieves. This man is a revolutionary bandit convicted of treason. This penitent man asks to be remembered by Jesus when he comes into his kingdom. Jesus goes him one better by telling him that long before the kingdom comes on earth as it is in heaven, long before the divine saving reign of God is fully manifest in this world, this zealot will be with Jesus in Paradise. It is interesting that apparently the only entrance requirement for this zealot is repentance of his sins and a trusting that Jesus is who he says, and thus a belief that Jesus is being wrongly crucified. The penitent man believes Jesus will indeed one day be a king reigning in his own kingdom and he wants to be a part of it, when the saints go marching in.

There is a bit of a controversy about where to place the word *today* in the sentence of Jesus' response to the bandit on the cross. Does Jesus mean "Truly I say to you today [i.e., I am telling you this truth today], you will be with me in Paradise" (at some undisclosed time in the future)? Or does Luke 23:43 mean, as seems much more likely, "Truly I say to you, today you will be with me in Paradise"? In English the difference is just a matter of whether you put the comma before or after the word *today*. The second suggested reading makes better sense. Jesus is contrasting a place later in his kingdom on earth with a place immediately in heaven with Jesus, which is where Jesus knows he is now going (see Luke 23:46: "Father, into your hands I commend my [human] spirit").

We turn now to Paul's discussion of heaven and hell, having gotten the gist of Jesus' perspective on the matter. What we will discover is that Paul has even less to say about heaven and hell than Jesus!

B. PAUL ON HEAVEN AND HELL

I was recently reading the very popular little book titled *90 Minutes in Heaven* by Don Piper.[1] Unlike near-death experiences, this is indeed a story of a man who was certified dead by the EMTs who responded to the emergency call about a horrendous wreck. There was no pulse, no heartbeat, no brain waves, no nothing for an hour and a half; he was simply left in the demolished car. There was also no lowering of his body temperature to preserve his brain cells, as the man was far from a hospital. He was in a Texas ditch! Even had it been less than half that amount of time, there would have been irreparable brain and heart damage, but there was none. We are talking a real miracle.

Don recounts the story of what happened to him while he was dead, namely, that he went straight to heaven, saw the gates, met various people he expected to be there, and heard what can only be called heavenly music. There was no tunnel, no light, no face of Jesus, just the things he mentioned. But suddenly he was wrenched back into this world where his mangled body had to be reassembled. He has spent years in pain and rehab. And he kept asking himself "Why?" Why would God bring him back from bliss to depression, suffering, and difficulties? The answer he came up with was this: in order to tell people how wonderful heaven will be. And Don now is in ministry in Texas, bolstered by that belief. In some ways Don's description of heaven, and the aftermath of seeing it, fits rather well with what Paul says in 2 Corinthians 12:

> I know a man in Christ who fourteen years ago (whether in the body I do not know, or out of the body I do not know, God knows) was caught up to the third heaven. And I know that such a man (whether in the body or apart from the body I do not know, God knows) was caught up into Paradise and heard inexpressible words, which a man is not permitted to speak.... Because of the surpassing greatness of the revelations, for this reason, to keep me from exalting myself, there was given me a thorn in the flesh, a messenger of Satan to torment me—to keep me from exalting myself! (vv. 2-7)

Paul glimpsed in a vision what Don Piper saw. Paul sees heaven as a place where all things become clear, where there are many revelations. The place itself can be described as being like Eden or paradise. In Galatians 4:26 he calls it "the Jerusalem above," in other words, a holy and heavenly city. This sort of combination we also see in Revelation 21–22, where John says that the heavenly Jerusalem will descend at the end of time and that the new creation on earth will involve not just a city, but a paradisiacal park or garden as well.

In 2 Corinthians 5:1-10 Paul gives a bit more description of what he has in view. He tells us that when a Christian dies he or she is absent from the body and present with the Lord. Whoever else there is to meet in heaven, the main thing is that Christ will be there and we will be present with him. The Bible doesn't promise reunion in heaven with any and all relatives or pets or friends. The Bible says that heaven is a place for the saints, for the believers in the biblical God; and more specifically in the New Testament, it is usually said to be the place for believers in Christ.

Second Corinthians 5:1-10 is interesting because Paul distinguishes three states of being: (1) we are clothed at present in this temporal and temporary dwelling that we call the body, which Paul likens to a tent; (2) when we die we leave the body behind, but that does not mean we cease to exist, nor does it mean we leave our "self" and personality behind. To the contrary, we go to be present with Christ. But Paul likens this to a state of nakedness, for we will have no body in heaven. But ... (3) he tells us that there will be an eternal dwelling for us, made without the help of human hands. He is referring to the resurrection body we will receive when Christ returns, and he expresses the desire that he would rather go straight from this body to the resurrection (an event he calls "being further clothed") than be stripped naked, have no body, and have to go into God's presence that way. Clearly, Paul would just as soon leave out the middle step of dying and being bodiless in heaven. He would rather go from the natural body straight to the resurrection body. The term *nakedness* in Paul's culture never connoted a preferable state of being.

And herein lies a clue as to why Paul says so very little about heaven. He sees it as only a *temporary* state of affairs, an interim condition until Christ and the saints return from heaven and believers get their resurrection bodies. Even when Paul contemplates his own demise in Philippians, and even though he sees going to be with Christ as preferable to continuing to suffer in this life (Phil. 1:23), his real and ultimate preference, the highest good he can contemplate, is resurrection. Here is what he says: "I want to know Christ and the power of his resurrection and the sharing of his sufferings by becoming like him in his death, if somehow I may attain the resurrection of the dead. Not that I have already obtained this or have already reached the goal, but I press on to make it mine" (Phil. 3:10-12). Notice that Paul does not think of his conversion or the new birth experience or his current life in Christ as "resurrection." No, resurrection is yet to come and Paul presses on to reach that goal, a goal where he sees himself finally fully conformed to the image of Christ, both in the flesh and inwardly as well—in heart and mind, in will and emotions. In Colossians, Paul puts it this way: "When Christ who is your life is revealed [i.e., at the second coming], then also you will be revealed with him in glory" (3:4). The glorious resurrection body will make us fully conformed to his image.

Does Paul have anything to add to our discussion of hell? As I already suggested, precious little, for Paul hardly discusses the matter at all. There is, however, one passage where we see clearly how Paul views the matter, 2 Thessalonians 1:5-9. Here Paul speaks of Christ returning to earth for judgment, in particular judgment on those who afflict the believers, which is expanded in verse 8 to include judgment on those who neither know God nor obey the gospel: "These will suffer the punishment of everlasting destruction, separated from the presence of the Lord and from the glory of his might" (v. 9).

This is hardly any more grim or dramatic than what Jesus says about Gehenna, but like what Jesus says, it has the same connotation of permanence and finality. The phrase "everlasting destruction" has puzzled some scholars—how can it be everlasting if it involves destruction? Yet the phrase is common enough (cf. 1 Thess. 5:3; 1 Cor. 5:5; 1 Tim. 6:9; and 4 Macc. 10:15). We could compare the reference to vessels who fit themselves for destruction in Romans 9:22 or the reference to eternal fire in Matthew 18:8 and 25:41. Everlasting destruction, then, is the opposite of everlasting life; and the phrase is meant to indicate a permanent state of affairs, not the annihilation of the person being judged. Compared to some Jewish apocalyptic sources Paul's language is actually quite mild, as he does not relish or dwell on the torments of the damned. He is mainly indicating just what Jesus did in his parable in Luke 16—they experience the permanent absence of the presence of God, and so the absence of bliss.

The imagery used here leads to a further point. Paul thinks that the holiness of the returning Christ will have two different effects on two different groups of people: one group it will judge and in some sense destroy; the other group it will purify and perfect. We are meant to think of the refiner's fire of a smelter, which burns away all the impurities in a piece of metal through the white-hot heat, but if the metal is left in the fire too long, it is destroyed. In both cases the change agent is exactly the same, but it has two different effects. C. S. Lewis once spoke of heaven as being too holy and bright for those who love dark deeds and darkness. They would never be comfortable there.

C. SATAN AND HIS MINIONS

The only book of the New Testament that gives us something of an extended discussion about Satan is the book of Revelation. He is of course referred to in Job 1–2 as "the satan," meaning the adversary, and he appears as a sort of prosecuting attorney from within and as a part of the heavenly court. The theology of Satan develops exponentially in the intertestamental period of early Judaism and then on into the New Testament period. In the Gospels we not only hear about Satan tempting Jesus in parallel accounts in Matthew 4 and Luke 4, but Jesus associates Satan with demons in Mark 3 during his debate with the Jewish authorities about the source of Jesus' power and authority to perform exorcisms.

At one juncture Jesus seems to suggest that Satan is working in and on Peter when he asks the question about his identity at Caesarea Philippi (Mark 8). Further, Jesus tells Peter at the Last Supper that Satan has asked to sift him and the other disciples; but Jesus, with greater power and authority, has told Peter that he has prayed and indicates he will recover from the test (Luke 22:31-32). At another juncture Jesus speaks of seeing Satan fall like lightning from the sky (Luke 10:18), a saying that is connected to the performance of exorcisms by Jesus' disciples. Clearly, Jesus sees his ministry as the harbinger of the demise of Satan. New Testament writers like Paul also see the death of Jesus as the beginning of the demise of the principalities and powers, which is to say the dark angels and forces that are aligned with and apparently under the spell of Satan (see Col. 2:15; Eph. 4:8).

When we talk about the locale of Satan he is always associated with the heavenly court, or with the air or sky; hence he is called "the prince of the power of the air" in Ephesians 2:2. He is also called by Jesus himself "the ruler of this world" (John 12:31; 14:30; 16:11). What we do not find in the New Testament is the notion that Satan has already been confined to some underworld place, some "hellhole," so to speak, but the book of Revelation expands all this language considerably. The ancient idea about hell being within or beneath the earth is not actually well grounded in the Bible.

In the book of Revelation there is an expansion or building on these sorts of ideas, and we hear about a threefold fall of Satan: from heaven to earth (Rev. 12), from earth to the pit (Rev. 20), and from the pit to the lake of fire (also Rev. 20). It is from this lake of fire image, and Jesus' depicting of Gehenna, that we get our notions that Satan is associated with hell. Interestingly, however, John of Patmos, the writer of Revelation, thinks Satan is not yet in hell or the lake of fire, and will not be there until the end of human history when he is finally judged by Christ.

Satan's story is, however, one of continual decline in the book of Revelation. In Revelation 12, when Satan attempts to seize Jesus the Messiah and destroy him (perhaps through Jesus' death), the text says that God snatches the Messiah up into heaven where Satan can do him no harm. Satan thus turns his attentions to the "Messiah's mother's" other offspring, namely believers. Human history is then seen as a struggle between the church and Satan, but the good news of Revelation 12 is that the "woman," who signifies the people of God, is given a place to which she may flee (the wilderness) and where she can be protected from Satan's repeated attacks. This is an image, not of the rapture of the church out of the world, but rather of its ongoing protection from annihilation within the world. Nevertheless, Satan is depicted as bewitching, bothering, and bewildering the church, bamboozling and seducing the world until his final demise at the return of Christ.

One New Testament depiction of Satan states: "Like a roaring lion, your adversary the devil prowls around looking for someone to devour. Resist him" (1 Pet. 5:8-9). In other words, Christians are not bulletproof from his attacks, so vigilance is required. Ephesians 6:10-17 sums up the peril of the situation, but also the provision for it in the gospel, quite well:

> Finally, be strong in the Lord and in the strength of his might. Put on the whole armor of God, that you may be able to stand against the schemes of the Devil. For we do not wrestle against flesh and blood, but against the rulers, against the authorities, against the cosmic powers over this present darkness, against the spiritual forces of evil in the heavenly places. Therefore take up the whole armor of God, that you may be able to withstand in the evil day, and having done all, to stand firm. Stand therefore, having fastened on the belt of truth, and having put on the breastplate of righteousness, and, as shoes for your feet, having put on the readiness given by the gospel of peace. In all circumstances take up the shield of faith, with which you can extinguish all the flaming darts of the evil one; and take the helmet of salvation, and the sword of the Spirit, which is the word of God.

There are adequate provisions for the Christian to be able to resist the temptations of Satan, here called the evil one and the devil. Notice that the forces of evil are said to be in the heavenly places (i.e., in the air or sky as opposed to in heaven itself, though the term *heaven* could refer to the lowest level of heaven), not in or under the earth. Notice as well that again Satan is seen not as some abstract evil force or power in the world, but as a supernatural personal being who has intentions, plans, schemes, and a will. James 4:7 reassures that whatever the powers of Satan, if the believer will resist him, he will flee.

The consistent witness of the New Testament is that Christians who have the spirit of God in their lives and Christ as Lord cannot be possessed by the devil. The devil may persecute or tempt the Christian, but not indwell him. This is an important note, and it means that there is no need for deliverance ministries practiced on genuine Christians. If Christ is Lord in their lives, there is not room for another lordship, and demonic possession is most definitely a form of lordship. This fact explains something else about the New Testament: There is next to no discussion about demonic possession once we get past the Gospels in the New Testament. It is barely mentioned in Acts 19:11-20 as something that can happen to non-Christians, but demonic possession per se is not really mentioned at all in Paul's letters or the other New Testament letters. This is because the consistent witness is that that sort of lordship cannot happen to a genuine Christian. Modern attempts to find demons as the source of all sorts of illnesses and problems in the Christian life have no basis in Scripture at all, and underestimate a fact that the New Testament continually reassures us of: "greater is he who is in you than he who is in this world" (1 John 4:4). Christians do not have to battle possession or internal demons in their lives. Indeed, the more one learns about the lordship of Christ over the powers and principalities, the more one realizes what we have been set free from.

There are several interesting texts that deal with the issue of Christ and the nefarious or evil powers in the world. It will serve us well to look at these texts together, but the background of them is crucial, namely, Genesis 6:1-4, the famous or infamous story of how the naughty fallen angels (called there "sons of God," a not uncommon epithet for angels) come down to earth and mate with the daughters of humankind, producing a race of giants! This exercise in crossbreeding is said to draw down the wrath of God on the earth in the form of Noah's flood. But back to those angels. This story absolutely fascinated early Jews and Christians. Inquiring minds longed to know what happened to those angels, and when and how were they judged?

Isaiah 24:21-22 reads: "On that day, the Lord will punish the hosts of heaven and on earth the kings of the earth. They will be gathered together like prisoners in a pit. They will be shut up in a prison, and after many days they will be punished." Notice that Isaiah distinguishes here between human kings and the hosts of heaven; these are two different groups. A passage written during the time between the writing of the Old Testament and the New Testament, 1 Enoch 10:4-6, reads "The Lord said to Raphael, 'Bind Azaz'el [clearly a demonic or evil supernatural figure if it is not Satan himself] hand and foot, throw him into the darkness!' And Raphael made a hole in the desert ... and cast him there; he threw on top of him rugged sharp rocks. And he covered his face in order that he might not see the light; and in order that he might be sent into the great fire on the day of judgment." With this background we can look at four New Testament references with greater understanding:

Jude (vs. 6)	2 Pet. (2:4)	1 Pet. (3:19-20)	Rev. (20:2-3)
And the angels	If God didn't	He went and	an angel…
who did not	spare the	made proclamation	with the key
keep their own	angels…but	to the spirits in	to the bottom
position he	cast them	prison who	bottomless
kept in chains	into Tartaros	formerly	pit and a
in deepest	in chains	disobeyed in	chain
darkness for	until	days of Noah.	Seized Satan
Judgment Day.	judgment.		bound him
			for 1000 years
			thrown into a
			pit

Even a brief examination of this material shows that it is inter-related, and all of it is indebted to the earlier Jewish material in Isaiah and probably Enoch as well. Here is the complete story: The fallen angels of Genesis 6:1-4 have been cast into a pit, a prison of sorts, awaiting Judgment Day. The same can be said to have happened to their boss—Satan. All await final judgment in those holding cells. But where are they? In *Tartaros* says 2 Peter, which means in outer darkness. In 1 Enoch this is said to be under the ground, which makes sense, but it might also be in the air. In any event, it becomes clear that 1 Peter 3:19-20, the most famous of these passages, is talking about the very same subject. The reference to the spirits who disobeyed in the times of Noah is a dead giveaway that the author has Genesis 6:1-4 clearly in view.

Therefore, the proclamation of Christ in 1 Peter 3:19-20 is not to human beings but rather to evil angels, and the proclamation presumably is of his victory over them by means of his death and resurrection, something we saw referred to in Colossians and Ephesians (see above). First Peter 3:19-20, therefore, has nothing to do with Christ descending into the land of the dead and preaching the gospel to the lost, nor does it have anything to do with a second-chance theology, something Jesus himself repudiated in his parable of the rich man and Lazarus. Final judgment, as it turns out, will involve judgment of the world, and the devil, and his minions. And the thrust of the New Testament about this whole matter is what Martin Luther once said: "One little word from Christ will fell him." The doom of Satan is sure.

In his wonderful book *The Screwtape Letters*, C. S. Lewis reminds us that we need to be careful to neither overestimate nor underestimate the powers of darkness. He says that the greatest trick of Satan is to create a smoke screen, which leads believers to think that Satan doesn't exist, or, if he does, he is a paper tiger, rather than a roaring lion. Both of these conclusions are errant judgments. Satan indeed, according to Revelation, is going to hell in a handbasket, or at least directly after a long stay in a dark and gloomy holding cell. His lackeys fare no better. Their doom is certain. But in the meantime, Satan and his minions are busy fighting a rearguard action against the church.

In a dramatic analogy, the New Testament scholar Oscar Cullmann once said that Christians today stand between D-Day, the turning point in the war (in this case, the war against the powers and principalities), and VE Day, when final judgment and victory have fully transpired. We live betwixt and between, or between the times. Satan is not yet confined or a spent force, but he knows he is running out of time and so are his underlings. This is why in the New Testament there are warnings about Satan and demons, but they are not given more credit or power than the situation warrants; and they are never said to be in control of the lives of Christians. We must consider a bit more closely Revelation at this point.

D. REVELATION—THE BOOK OF MARTYRS

If we look carefully at the whole of the book of Revelation, its major message is that *though Christians are being persecuted, prosecuted, and in some cases executed, God is still in control of this world; and in the end justice and redemption will be wrought upon the earth.* The kingdoms of this world will become the kingdoms of our God and of his Christ. And because this book stresses the sovereignty of God, it also stresses the theme "vengeance is mine, I will repay." Retribution and justice issues should be left in God's hands according to the writer, John of Patmos. And so Jesus Christ calls his converts in the seven churches to be prepared for suffering and martyrdom. Why should they not prepare to retaliate? Because, as the crucial vision in Revelation 5 makes clear, only the Lamb is worthy to unleash judgments on humankind. Only the Lamb has the knowledge and compassion to dole out justice tempered properly with mercy. And it is crucial to note that the judgments described in the three sets of sevens are not punitive but disciplinary. They are meant to be reality checks intended to lead the world to get on its knees and get right with God. Final judgment does not come until after Christ returns to earth.

Final judgment, furthermore, has nothing to do with battles between Middle Eastern foes or European foes now or in the future. As Revelation 20:7-10 makes perfectly clear, there will be no final Armageddon battle. Instead, there will just be an execution. Fire will come down from heaven and the evil armies will be consumed. Revelation 19:14-16 gives a preview of this, and the outcome is no different—the sword of the Lord will strike down the wicked nations. "He will tread the winepress of the fury of the wrath of God, the Almighty" (19:15), and notice that the only armies fighting for and with him are the "armies of heaven" (19:14).

This has nothing whatsoever to do with modern politics and international relationships. It has to do with world affairs *after* Christ returns to judge the living and the dead. Nothing that is happening now in human history can force this return of Christ to transpire any sooner or later than God decides. None of the events transpiring now lead up to the return of Christ in such a fashion that we could read the signs of the times and tell when it will happen. On the contrary, Christ will come like a thief in the night. The book of Revelation should sound the death knell of all idle speculations about the timing of the final eschatological events, since they are all triggered by the return of the rider on the white horse, the Christ, the Son of God. Judgment lies in his hands and in no other's.

This fact—that judgment is and should be left in the hands of God in Christ—is at one and the same time both frustrating and reassuring. To the saints to whom John wrote it must have been tremendously comforting, for they were a tiny minority without armies or governments to back or protect them. For some modern Americans, it will be seen as frustrating, because it means that Christians are called to not place their hands on the levers of power and destruction, not put their fingers on the triggers even though they can do so, but rather to learn to leave such matters in the hands of God. The book of Revelation, though full of judgments, is not a call to "get ready to rumble!" It is not a call to arms at all; rather, it is just the opposite. John tells us: "Say a farewell to arms, and trust in the Lamb who alone is worthy to unseal the seals and dole out judgments both preliminary and final, both disciplinary and punitive upon the earth." The book of Revelation's message to Christians, then and now, is a message of preparation for martyrdom, not a call to be ready to kill, but a call to be ready to die, and not for any nationalistic or cultural cause, but for one's Christian faith.

The Reformers, perhaps particularly Calvin, were uncertain not only why Revelation was in the Bible at all but what to do with it. It is the only New Testament book Calvin wrote no commentary on. Even so, on further review a close reading of Revelation tells us that this book has a message that comports with the message of Jesus in the Sermon on the Mount. Christians are called to nonviolence, to nonresistance, and to deeds of piety and charity. The only army they are urged to join by this book is one that we might call the Salvation Army, the army of proclaimers of Christ's redemption, the army of witnesses and martyrs. It is no accident that martyrs receive special places in heaven (under the altar in Rev. 6:9) and in the millennium by Christ's side (Rev. 20:4). Long before there was a Foxe's *Book of Martyrs* (one of the most popular early Protestant works, written by John Foxe [1516–1587]), there was the book of Revelation, meant to provide hope and reassurance to those suffering and those being persecuted and even executed. And the message to all such folk is clear: The slain Lamb is your model of behavior. He alone is worthy to judge the earth, so trust in the sovereignty of Christ and be prepared, if need be, to follow his example, even unto death.

E. AND SO?

When I was small, I once asked my grandfather, who lived in Wilmington, North Carolina, why he was such a straight arrow. Why did he work so hard as a fire chief, why was he a deacon in the Baptist Church, why did he volunteer to count ballots at elections for no pay, why did he live such a good and godly life? His reply was instantaneous: "Because heaven is too sweet and hell too hot to mess around in this life." In other words, his credo was determined by keeping his eye on the finish line, on life's goal. Scholars call this the use of an eschatological sanction to undergird a biblical ethic of life and lifestyle.

The author of Revelation, however, saw that the ultimate sanction lay not merely in the existence of heaven or hell, however vividly and vibrantly he describes it, but in a sovereign God who will one day return in the person of his Son to earth to judge the living and the dead. Indeed, according to 2 Corinthians 5:10, he will judge the deeds of Christians also. There will be a final reckoning, a final accounting for the deeds done in the body, and there is no reason to doubt that Christians will be held to a higher standard of accountability since they have been given a higher ethical code by which to live.

Justice, in the end, is not done by believers' simply dying and going to be with the Lord. The God of the Bible is a holy God, a God of righteousness and justice, and so the book of Revelation makes evident that justice must be done finally on the face of the earth. The saints under the altar in heaven in Revelation 6 ask the appropriate question: "How long, O Lord, must evil prevail upon the earth?" How long must martyrdoms go on? The answer is that the Lamb has the matter in hand. But we should be careful what we wish and pray for.

When we pray "thy kingdom come on earth as it is in heaven," we are praying for no more time for amendment of life. We are praying for no more opportunity for repentance. We are praying for what C. S. Lewis is referring to when he says, "When the author [of the divine play] walks on to the stage [of human history] the play is over." Indeed, and he shall reign forever and ever, not merely somewhere out there, but down here as well on the earth, first in the millennium and then in the new heaven and the new earth. But how can we reign with Christ on earth if we have died? Resurrection is the answer, as we will soon see.

CHAPTER 4

RAISING THE DEAD

Make no mistake: if He rose at all
it was as His body;
if the cells' dissolution did not reverse, the molecules
    reknit, the amino acids rekindle,
the Church will fall.
It was not as the flowers,
each soft Spring recurrent;
it was not as His Spirit in the mouths and fuddled
    eyes of the eleven apostles;
it was as His Flesh: ours....
Let us not mock God with metaphor,
analogy, sidestepping, transcendence;
making of the event a parable, a sign painted in the
    faded credulity of earlier ages:
let us walk through the door....
Let us not seek to make it less monstrous,

> *for our own convenience, our own sense of beauty,*
> *lest, awakened in one unthinkable hour, we are*
>   *embarrassed by the miracle,*
> *and crushed by remonstrance.*
> —John Updike, "Seven Stanzas at Easter"

When John Updike wrote this poem in 1960, it was fashionable in some theological circles either to deny that Jesus rose in the flesh or to suggest it was merely some sort of visionary experience the disciples had, rather than something that actually happened to Jesus. Updike, as the poem indicates, was having none of it. He understood something often missed in the discussion—the actual meaning of the term *resurrection* in early Judaism. The term *resurrection*, even when it is used for metaphorical purposes such as in Ezekiel 37, always refers to something that happens to a physical body after its demise. It does not refer to some sort of spiritual experience or to dying and going to heaven, nor does it ever refer to something that happened to someone *else* other than the deceased. All this has been clearly established by the good bishop of Durham, N. T. Wright.[1]

Paul himself makes this emphatically clear by using the Greek phrase "resurrection from out of the dead ones" (Phil. 3:11) in referring to what happened to Jesus and his body on Easter. He had been dead and buried, but on the third day what happened was that God raised him up from out of the realm of the dead persons such that his physical body was no longer in the grave; indeed, it was transformed. He had been truly dead and was truly alive once more, due to a miracle. For Jews like Jesus, or the Pharisees of his day, resurrection was proof positive that the end times had come to pass. We need to discuss resurrection at some length, and perhaps the best place to start is by considering what resurrection is not.

A. RESURRECTION IS NOT REINCARNATION, GOING TO HEAVEN, OR IMMORTALITY OF THE SOUL

I was in a hurry to get to a little Methodist Chapel near Durham, England. I was scheduled to preach there on Easter morning and my bus arrived late. As I raced up the hill, down the hill running came the chapel steward, all red in the face. He stopped abruptly in front of me and said, "I'm ever so sorry, but I must ask you a question." I replied, "Shoot." He looked flustered and said, "No, nothing so drastic as shooting, I simply need to know: You do believe in the resurrection of Jesus, don't you?" I in turn replied, "Of course. That's what I am here to proclaim." The relief on the man's face was evident. He added, "I'm ever so glad, as the chap we had last Easter didn't, and he went on endlessly about the beauty of the return of spring and the flowers."

People do sometimes have strange ideas as to what Easter is really about, so let's say here that resurrection has nothing to do with: (1) the cycle of the seasons and crops; (2) the Far Eastern notion of reincarnation; (3) the Greco-Roman idea of the immortality of the soul; and finally, (4) the Christian idea of dying and going to heaven. All these ideas are interesting ways of thinking about the afterlife, but they should not be confused with the New Testament and early Jewish idea of resurrection.

Let's tackle first of all the mistaken association of resurrection with the crop cycle and spring. I suppose it is somewhat natural to make such an association since Jesus rose in April A.D. 30, right at the cusp of a Judean spring season. But in fact resurrection is not a cyclical event that happens regularly like spring, nor is the story of Jesus' rising from the dead about a *natural* occurrence. The resurrection is a historical event that happened to a human being, not a cyclical natural occurrence involving plants. It has nothing to do with the coming of spring and the natural sort of new life it brings.

Life goes through a series of incarnations. In one life you may start as a bird, move up to being a lion in the next life, and then become a human being. Or if you have bad karma (your bad deeds that carry over from your previous life), you may well go in a retrograde direction—start as a human and end up like Kafka's bug! The basic idea here is that all life is connected, an idea that the Bible does not support, especially when it comes to human beings. In the Bible, human beings are created in the image of God. Each one is unique and of sacred worth and in no way connected to other life-forms, be they plants or animals. Indeed, each individual human being maintains his or her unique identity throughout all eternity in the Christian way of thinking. In the resurrection Bob will still be Bob, Mary will still be Mary, and so on. Resurrection is something that happens to individual persons, who each continue to have the same personal identity thereafter.

More confusing to some is the issue of the relationship between the immortality of the soul and the resurrection of the body, because Christians in the early Middle Ages tried to blend the two views of the afterlife together. Christians regularly began talking about their immortal souls and have done so ever since, even though the New Testament says nothing about it.

Don't get me wrong, the New Testament says plenty about the afterlife. But when it wants to talk about being "absent from the body and present with the Lord," (2 Cor. 5:8), it doesn't use the word *soul*; rather, *spirit*, the human spirit, is referred to. Remember Jesus' words from the cross in Luke 23:46—"Into thy hands I commend my spirit"? Jews who were not strongly influenced by Greco-Roman ideas did not affirm the concept of an immortal soul—a soul that had and would always exist, and was inherently immortal or eternal. The Greeks talked about the immortal soul as imprisoned in the body, and in fact with the rise of asceticism in the second through the fourth centuries, Christians began to see the body in a negative light and adopted and adapted the terminology of the immortal soul.

The problem, of course, with this whole way of thinking is that the Bible affirms that everlasting life is a gift from God, received through faith. It's not an inherent property of some part of every human being called the "soul." The term *psuche* in the New Testament really shouldn't be translated "soul," as it usually refers to our natural life breath. Thus, for example, when Paul in

1 Corinthians 15 talks about the first Adam, he refers to God breathing into him and his becoming a body with breath in it, a living being. This has nothing to do with some nonmaterial part of a human that Greeks called the soul. It has to do with simply being alive with natural life breath in us. In any case, none of this has anything to do with resurrection, which does not have to do with our spirits so much as it has to do with our bodies. It was not the spirit of Jesus that needed resurrection. His spirit could just go on to heaven and be with the Father. No, it was his dead body that was the issue, and resurrection was the means by which that body went from being a corpse to being the risen Jesus.

What about dying and going to heaven? Certainly the New Testament has something to say on this subject. It affirms that the Christian person survives death; and as 2 Corinthians 5 puts it, the naked spirit of a person goes to be with the Lord, while the body remains in the ground. One could also compare the famous parable of the rich man and Lazarus in Luke 16, but caution has to be exercised, since it is a parable and not meant to be a literal description of the afterlife. What it nevertheless shows is that Jesus did believe that the human spirit survived death, went somewhere, and was still conscious thereafter. What it also shows is that Jesus believed this life is the time and place of decision. The choices we make here and now are said in this parable to have everlasting consequences, which cannot be altered after the fact.

The book of Revelation makes equally clear that when Christians die they do go to be with the Lord; they do go to heaven. But it must also be said that only about 5 percent of the discussion about the afterlife in the New Testament focuses on heaven or hell. Ninety-five percent focuses, not on the other world, but rather on the afterlife and, more specifically, on resurrection. Now that we know what resurrection is not, we will consider what the New Testament writers did mean by resurrection.

B. JESUS ON THE RESURRECTION

I am not an archaeologist, nor do I play one on TV, but if I were, the thing I would most love to discover is the gravestone of Lazarus. In my imagination it would read as follows: "Died A.D. 29," and then below that, "Died again A.D. 42." This ought to confuse some folks. Perhaps one of the most confusing things about resurrection is why Jesus' resurrection is seen as the first one by New Testament writers. Why, exactly, does Paul call Jesus the firstfruits up from the dead? Had he not read the stories in the Old Testament about Elijah raising someone from the dead? What about the Gospel stories of Jesus raising Lazarus, or the widow of Nain's son, or the daughter of Jairus? Weren't those resurrections too?

These are perfectly good questions, and they deserve a good answer. The answer the Bible suggests is that yes, each of these persons was genuinely dead and genuinely raised from the dead; but no, they did not receive a resurrection body in the process of being raised back to life on this earth. They came back to a mortal condition. They reinhabited a body prone to disease, decay, and death. This is not the case with Jesus. He is the first to receive the eschatological or resurrection body immune to disease, decay, and death. This is why Paul calls him the firstfruits of the resurrection.

But what did Jesus himself say about resurrection? Even that is unclear. John 11 reports Jesus saying, "I am the resurrection and the life." Whatever this means, it cannot mean "I already have a resurrection body." More likely, Jesus is speaking metaphorically. He means that, like the Father, he is the source of life and resurrection; and Martha does not need to wait until the end of time for the raising of her brother. It can happen right now, because to be in the presence of Jesus is to be in the presence of Life itself, the Life-Giver. But Jesus is also perfectly capable of talking about resurrection in a literal sense, both his own resurrection and that of others. Let's start with what he says about others first.

Tucked away in the middle of John 5 are these words of Jesus: "Truly, truly I say to you the hour is coming, and is now here, when the dead will hear the voice of the Son of God and will live.... The hour is coming when all those who are in their graves will come out—those who have done good to the resurrection of life, and those who have done evil to the resurrection of condemnation" (vv. 25, 28-29). Obviously, to be raised from the dead doesn't necessarily entail ending up having a wonderful everlasting life. Resurrection is what happens prior to the final judgment and the separating of those who rise to life and those who rise to condemnation.

Early Jews did indeed have a concept of the resurrection of the righteous or the just being something different from the resurrection of the condemned. We actually see this in 1 Corinthians 15, where Paul says that when Christ returns, only those who died as Christians will be raised immediately. This in turn leads us to a text like Revelation 20, which tells us that the resurrection of believers happens at the beginning of the millennial reign of Christ on the earth, whereas the resurrection of the unrighteous comes at the end of that period of time. Resurrection is no guarantee of a happy afterlife. You want to be in the first resurrection when Jesus returns to ensure that outcome.

What is interesting, and indeed novel, about Jesus' discussions concerning his own resurrection is that he does not see it as happening as part of the resurrection of the righteous at the end of human history. To the contrary, he suggests his resurrection will be something unique, standing out like an isolated miracle not long after his death. He puts it this way some three times in Mark 8–10: "The Son of Man must suffer many things and be killed and after three days arise" (cf. Mark 8:31; 9:31; 10:34). It would be understandable that if Jesus said this without further explanation, his disciples would assume he was telling them that he would come back the same way Lazarus came back from the dead, and life would go on very much as it had before then. But in fact what happened at Easter to Jesus is that he did not go back to business as usual, he did not go back to his former condition and former tasks. Rather, he went forward into an eschatological condition with a body immune to disease, decay, and death.[2]

Paul tries to encapsulate the differences when he speaks in

Romans 1:3-4 of "the gospel concerning his Son, who was descended from David according to the flesh, and was vindicated to be Son of God in power by means of the Spirit of holiness, by resurrection from the dead, Jesus Christ our Lord." At the resurrection Jesus became the risen Lord; he became Son of God in power, whereas previously he had been Son of God in weakness and human vulnerability. Jesus, like the Pharisees, believed in resurrection in the flesh, but what happened to that flesh on Easter was far more than either the Pharisees had expected or Jesus had announced. There was a surprise element in Easter. We will understand this better if we turn to Paul's views on things.

C. PAUL'S VIEWS ON RESURRECTION

In the longest exposition we have on resurrection in the New Testament, 1 Corinthians 15, Paul lays out just exactly how he views the matter of continuity and discontinuity between the lives and bodies we have now, and the lives and bodies of those in Christ at the resurrection. We will focus on 1 Corinthians 15:42-49. The element of continuity between who we are now and who we will be then is threefold: (1) each of us will be the same person—and personality; (2) in a body; and (3) with life.

Paul, however, places the emphasis on the discontinuity between the bodies we now have and the ones we shall have. The current body is weak, inglorious, perishable, and physical. The bodies we will receive will be powerful, glorious, imperishable, and "spiritual." But what does that last word mean here? Is Paul saying the resurrection body is an immaterial one? No, in fact he is not. He draws a contrast between the first Adam and the last one, the first one having merely life breath in a body, whereas the last one, Christ, became a life-giving spirit at the resurrection. The phrase "spiritual body," which occurs in verse 44, refers to a real, tangible body that is totally empowered by the Holy Spirit, just as the first Adam's body was not made of natural air or life breath but rather was empowered or animated by it. The contrast is between a natural "life breath"–empowered body and a Spirit-empowered one. Paul believes that at the resurrection we will become like Christ in the flesh. Just as Christ became a person who could dispense the Spirit at the resurrection since he was totally empowered by the Spirit, so also at the resurrection we become totally empowered by the Spirit. Merely mortal flesh and blood is left behind, but everlasting flesh is what we are given instead.

D. AND SO?

Perhaps here is a good point to make an important distinction. There is a difference between everlasting life and eternal life, though sometimes we use the terms as if they were interchangeable. The biblical view of human life is that life begins at conception. It did not exist before that point in time. Thus when we talk about the gift we are given both spiritually and physically by Christ and his Spirit, strictly speaking it should be called everlasting life—a life that begins at a particular point in time and that goes forward into eternity, never ending thereafter. Eternal life, by contrast, a life that always was, is, and will be, is something only God has ever had or will ever have. The concept of resurrection reminds us that we are not inherently immortal beings. We began somewhere in time, and if we are to have a positive everlasting life, raised from the dead, this too is a gift from God, not an inherent human property or some kind of birthright. Jesus is the Life, and we are not. To the extent we are in him, we have everlasting life and have it abundantly.

The rabbis used to speculate, of course, about what the nature of life in the resurrection would be like. Some thought that in the resurrection we would be raised from the dead at our optimum age, the age when we were most vital and alive. Some thought that those who had lost their hair and teeth would regain them. There is even a humorous discussion about how the lost would be gnashing their teeth in the afterlife if they had no teeth. The rebuttal was that in the resurrection those condemned would be given teeth and a voice box so they could lament and gnash their teeth in Gehenna! What such discussions show is that early Jews, who did believe in resurrection (although there were Jews, like the Sadducees, who did not believe in the resurrection) believed that resurrection meant something that happened to a body.

If we go back to the Easter stories in the four Gospels, these stories are all about a Jesus who is the same—in that he is tangible, can eat, has a physical body—and yet different, for he can suddenly appear in and disappear from a location. Paul says the same thing when he tries to lay out the continuity and discontinuity between our present bodies and the resurrection body. *Most important, we learn from 1 Corinthians 15 that Christ's history is our destiny.* We are the Easter people. And if we are in Christ, one day we will share a resurrection body like the one he had on the first Easter. The earliest Christians believed that Easter was just the beginning of the end times. Near the end of the end times, when Jesus returned, he would do unto others what had been done unto him—raise them from the dead.

In the next chapter, we turn to a discussion about what happens after the resurrection.

CHAPTER 5

THE AFTERLIFE—THE RAP-TURE, THE MILLENNIUM, AND THE NEW HEAVEN AND THE NEW EARTH

If the lives of men can be measured in terms of years, ide-ologies in decades, and nations in centuries, then the unit measuring civilizations, born of the interaction among peo-ples, would be the millennium. —Abdelaziz Bouteflika

Unfortunately since the early nineteenth century, the discus-sion of Revelation 20–22 has been done under the presence of an ominous dark cloud called the rapture. This is so much the case that some have just thrown up their hands and thrown out the discussion of the millennium because of its supposed associations with the rapture doctrine. It was not always so, but in order to clear the air and chase away those ominous clouds, we will speak first about the rapture doctrine, a subject already introduced in our earlier discussion of 1 Thessalonians 4–5.

A. THE ORIGIN OF THE SPECIOUS—THE RAPTURE NOTION[1]

In 1830 in Glasgow, Scotland, a young girl named Margaret MacDonald attended a healing service. She was said to have received a vision on the occasion of a two-stage return of Christ, though it is not clear whether she envisioned a pre-tribulation or a post-tribulation rapture to coordinate with the first of these comings. The matter might have fallen into obscurity except that a British Evangelical preacher named John Nelson Darby heard the story and spread it far and wide. Darby was to become the founder of the Plymouth Brethren denomination. He explained more fully and clearly that Christ would definitely come twice, the first in secret to rapture the church out of the world and up to heaven. He would then return after seven years of worldwide tribulation to establish a dominion on earth based in Jerusalem. Darby coordinated this latter event with the discussion of the "glorious appearing" referred to in Titus 2:13 and distinguished it from the discussion of the parousia in 1 Thessalonians 4.

The term *rapture* does not occur anywhere in the New Testament. It comes from the Latin word *raptio*, which in turn is a translation of the Greek word that means "caught up" (1 Thess. 4:17). For both Darby and later dispensationalists, the most important scriptural basis for the notion of a "rapture" was 1 Thessalonians 4, and we have already seen in this study that 1 Thessalonians 4, while certainly talking about meeting Christ in the air when he returns, is not about a rapture into heaven at some supposed secret coming of Christ. The event in 1 Thessalonians 4 is clearly enough portrayed as a loud and very public event; indeed, as a royal return and welcome.

The teaching of the rapture might still have remained a relatively obscure matter confined to one small Protestant group in the British Isles, except for the fact that Darby made numerous evangelistic trips to America between 1859 and 1877 and won many American converts to his rapture theology. Note carefully the dates of these trips. Darby showed up on the brink of the Civil War, during the war, and after the war, right when many Americans were quite vulnerable to escapist thinking that promised they would not have to go through a great tribulation. The timing could not have been better for promulgating such a theology.

To his credit, Darby refrained from going for the jackpot of predicting specific dates for the end of the world, the rapture, or the visible second coming of Christ. What he did instead was to invent "dispensations," by which was meant intervals in God's timetable of eschatological events that he coordinated with various texts and prophecies. Darby concluded that God had divided all of history into seven distinct dispensations, or ages. In each of these dispensations God dealt with people differently with differing rules.

Again, the matter might have been a flash in the pan, except for two further developments. Dwight L. Moody became enamored with this theology and began promulgating it on both sides of the Atlantic, a theology that was to be furthered by the founding of the Moody Bible Institute, and eventually by Moody Press and by a radio network. But by far the single most enduring tool for spreading this theology was a reference Bible, put together by one Cyrus I. Scofield, first published in 1909.

The *Scofield Reference Bible* had both the King James Version text and extensive notes throughout coupled with maps, charts, and dispensation headings. Most of the major prophetic texts had comments, which coordinated with one or another of the dispensations according to Darby's teachings. The headings and notes were woven into the text itself, which made it appear as though this teaching were self-evident and indeed arose directly from the Bible. With the publication of this Bible, Scofield hit the jackpot, selling millions. What few know about him today is that he was an embezzler and a forger, who abandoned his wife and children and did time in jail even after his apparent conversion to Christianity.[2] But never mind all this, his Bible had a life of its own, due in large part to the promotion of the Moody Bible Institute and a wealthy Chicago businessman named William E. Blackstone, who himself had already cashed in on the rapture in 1878 writing the book *Jesus Is Coming* (veiling his identity by simply having the initials W. E. B. appended to the book and its title page). Blackstone was an avid Zionist, and his book helped further the fervor for studying Scripture in light of this sort of prophetic schema.

There was, however, a major problem that needed to be addressed. Despite the ever-growing popularity of this theology with American laypeople, frightened by one war or another, this theology did not have any basis. It did not arise out of detailed study of the biblical text in its original languages. Indeed, it was dependent in many ways on the King James translation of the Bible.[3]

It is certainly not surprising, then, that someone like Lewis Chafer, a Presbyterian, would come along feeling the need to establish a dispensationalist training center, in part to shore up the liabilities of dispensationalist theology. The result was Dallas Theological Seminary, founded in 1924, which produced John Walvoord (who was president of the institution between 1952 and 1986), Charles Ryrie, Hal Lindsey, and many names familiar to readers of Evangelical theology. It is these leaders and their writings that impacted Jerry Falwell, Pat Robertson, Timothy and Beverley LaHaye, Reverend John Hagee, and a host of dispensationalist televangelists.

In the wake of the enormous success of the best-selling books in the Left Behind series and in view of the biblical illiteracy of our culture and even the church, it is not surprising this way of thinking continues to be popular. American Christians are looking for the theological equivalent of comfort food and escapist entertainment, and dispensationalist theology readily meets those needs. But we need to closely examine whether this is a true version or a perversion of what the Bible actually teaches. Only detailed attention to the biblical text can answer such questions.

It is easy enough to show the problems in dispensationalist theology when it comes to a text like Revelation 4:1-2: "After this I looked, and there before me was a door standing open in heaven. And the voice I had first heard speaking to me like a trumpet said, 'Come up here, and I will show you what must take place after this.' And at once I was in the Spirit, and there before me was a throne."

This is not a description of a magic-carpet ride to heaven taken by John of Patmos. It is a description of a visionary experience, as is true of the whole rest of Revelation. John "in the Spirit" is enabled to see into heaven, to take a tour of what is happening there, and to see into the future. This description is much like that which we find in other apocalyptic literature that uses this sort of metaphorical language. Notice, for example, Revelation 17:3: "Then the angel carried me away in the Spirit into the desert." Once again John has not left the rock pile known as Patmos. It is "in the Spirit" that he is transported and sees a desert scene. This is a way of talking about a visionary experience.

Another favorite text to prove that the "rapture" is biblical is Matthew 24:29-44. The context of the discussion is the events that surround the coming of the Son of Man from heaven, which will include cosmic signs of distress (v. 29) that make the idea of this coming being secret or clandestine far-fetched. Indeed, we are told that once the sign of the Son of Man appears in the heavens, all the nations of the earth will see it and mourn (v. 30). He will come on the clouds with power, glory, and angels (vv. 30-31). Verse 37 makes it perfectly clear that the very same second coming is in view in verses 37-41. The discussion is still about the coming of the Son of Man, and the material in verses 29-31 refers to the same event described in verses 37-41.

An analogy is drawn between the days of Noah and the days of the end. The issue has to do with what is meant by "one is taken, and the other left" (vv. 40-41). Two things need to be said: First, those who were "taken away" in the days of Noah were swept away by the flood and so are judged. Second, in terms of the oppressive situation during Jesus' own day, when someone was "taken," they were indeed being taken away by the authorities for judgment. It was the ones left behind who were fortunate. And this is in fact what verses 40-41 mean in their original context. Being "taken," whether in Noah's day or in Jesus', was not a favorable outcome—it meant judgment. Notice as well that there is no reference to the person taken being taken up or being taken to heaven. This text has nothing to do with such an idea. But the heart and soul of the case for the rapture, whether pre-tribulation, mid-tribulation, or post-tribulation, is of course 1 Thessalonians 4–5 and, to a lesser degree, 2 Thessalonians 2.

Paul saw himself as both a prophetic interpreter of the sayings of the historical Jesus and of the Old Testament and also someone who received direct messages from the risen Lord himself. In 1 Thessalonians 4:15–5:7, Paul does draw on the Jesus tradition found in Matthew 24, but in verses 16-17 he also draws on both his own reading of Daniel and prophetic insight that he himself had been given by the risen Lord. The following chart shows the various parallels:

	1 Thessalonians	Matthew
Christ returns	4:16	24:30
from heaven	4:16	24:30
accompanied by angels	4:16	24:31
with a trumpet of God	4:16	24:31
believers gathered to	4:17	24:31, 40-41
Christ		
in clouds	4:17	24:30
time unknown	5:1-2	24:36
coming like a thief	5:2, 4	24:43
unbelievers unaware of	5:3	24:37-39
coming judgment		
judgment like a mother's	5:3	24:8
birth pangs		
believers not deceived	5:4-5	24:43
believers to be watchful	5:6	24:37-39
warning vs. drunkenness	5:7	24:49

These parallels should not be minimized, and they make it likely that Paul is drawing on the general sense, trajectory, and imagery of some of that material from the sayings of Jesus. They also make clear this important point: Paul does not think there is some difference between the parousia and the second coming (or glorious appearing). Indeed, as in Matthew 24, all of this material is referring to one event—the coming of the Son of Man on the clouds. Notice that the parallels with Matthew 24 continue on into 1 Thessalonians 5:1-11. This is because Paul does not think he is describing a different event in 1 Thessalonians 5:1-11 than he was in 1 Thessalonians 4:13-18. We can say with even more assurance that the reason he uses the phrase "word of the Lord" (1 Thess. 4:15) is to console and reassure the church about the fate of their deceased loved ones.

B. THE BOOK OF DANIEL AS BACKGROUND

Daniel 7:13-14 is part of the famous oracle about "the one like a son of man" (*bar enasha*). Though it has been debated whether this figure goes up into the clouds and heaven to meet the Ancient of Days or comes with the clouds to meet the Almighty on earth for the day of judgment, in view of verse 14, it must surely be the latter. It is the kingdoms "under heaven" that are handed over to the Son of Man and to the saints, and we are told all rulers will worship and obey this figure. It is surely not envisioned that these non-Jewish kingdoms and rulers are in heaven or are ruled from heaven. Ruling, like the final judgment, takes place on earth. Notice as well the statement that the Son of Man comes with the clouds of heaven—an image of clouds come down from above. The clouds do not rise up from the earth with someone ascending with them.

This background material is important for another reason. Daniel 7 is about this Son of Man ruling over those who had oppressed God's people on earth. It is not about rescuing God's people out of this world into heaven for an interim period of time. The Son of Man language and imagery taken over from

Daniel 7, in the sayings of Jesus in Matthew 24 and here by Paul in 1 Thessalonians, provide further proof that 1 Thessalonians 4:13-18 is not about a rapture.

Daniel 12:1 speaks of a major distress "at that time" from which God's people will be delivered. This is followed in verse 2 by the promise that multitudes "who sleep in the dust of the earth shall awake, some to everlasting life, others to everlasting shame and everlasting contempt." It seems very likely that Paul has some of this material in mind in 1 Thessalonians 4–5; although, typically, as he does with the Jesus tradition, Paul has made the material his own, using his own way of phrasing things.

C. PAUL ON THE AFTERLIFE

In 1 Thessalonians 5, the message of the material relating to the end times is a bit different from that in 1 Thessalonians 4. Rather than for consolation, this chapter is more about admonition based on the knowledge the audience already has. This section seems to have three divisions, and the markers of each involve the word *but*: (1) "but concerning"—5:1; (2) "but you"—5:4; and (3) "but we"—5:8. Paul deals with three related topics in these sections: (1) the sudden, and for some unexpected, coming of the Day of the Lord when unbelievers will be judged (5:1-3), (2) the preparation of believers for that day (5:4-7), and (3) the necessary faithfulness of God's people, all of which form the basis for encouraging one another (5:8-11).

It is a helpful exercise to compare what is said here in this whole passage with Romans 13:11-14. There are obvious similarities in the use of the language about waking, sleeping, and sobriety. If any one of these passages conveys more of a sense that the eschatological clock is ticking and the end may be nearer than one thinks, it is surely the Romans passage. There is really no evidence that Paul's views about the end times change, because Romans was written after 2 Corinthians; and yet Paul is still talking about the possibly imminent return of Christ.

Both 1 Thessalonians 5:1-11 and 1 Thessalonians 4:13-18 deal with the one and only return of Christ from slightly different angles, both commending the same sort of behavior by Christians in light of the end times. The exhortations in 1 Thessalonians 5:1-11 are pointless if in fact believers were not envisioned as still on earth until the Day of the Lord. Notice the repetition of the phrase "with the Lord" in verses 4:17 and 5:10 and the similar endings directed toward the immediate audience in 4:18 and 5:11. The context and the content of these passages indicate that Paul is speaking of the one and only second coming in them both. What is not usually appreciated is, while the former passage examines the second coming from the angle of the coming rescue of believers, the latter passage examines the same event from the perspective of judgment on unbelievers.

The important phrase in 1 Thessalonians 5:1, "times and kind of times" (*chronoi kai kairoi*), is found elsewhere in early Jewish and early Christian literature (Acts 1:7; 1 Pet. 1:11; Ignatius *Poly.* 3 cf.; Neh. 10:34; 13:31; Dan. 2:21; Wisd. of Sol. 8:8; Eccl. 3:1; and Demosthenes, *Olynth.* 3 para. 32). *Chronos*, from which we get the word *chronology*, refers more to the quantity of time, while *kairos* refers to the quality of time. *Kairos* also carries a sense of a brief, propitious moment. The gist of the phrase "times and kind of times" is that the audience has no need to be informed about how long must elapse before the big event happens or what significant occurrences will mark or punctuate that crucial occasion. Paul refuses to set up timetables for this event, because he cannot do so.[4] The timing has *not* been revealed. Indeed, what has been revealed is that no one knows the timing of this event, not even Jesus during his ministry (Mark 13:32). All the pointless speculation about the timing of the rapture or the return of Christ is an exercise in futility because the former event is not going to happen, and we are told that the latter event will happen at a hitherto undisclosed time.

First Thessalonians 5:2 then tells us nothing about when Jesus will come, but rather how—in a sudden and unexpected manner. Paul is describing a sudden intrusion into human history, catching many unaware and unprepared. As we have already discovered, the metaphor "thief in the night" goes back to Jesus and the early church (cf. Matt. 24:43; Luke 12:38-39; 1 Thess. 5:2; 2 Pet. 3:10; Rev. 3:3; 16:15), and it stresses both the suddenness and the unexpectedness of the event, but also its unknown timing. It also has an aura of threat for the unprepared.

Paul uses several related phrases to refer to this coming event—the Day (1 Thess. 5:4; 1 Cor. 3:13; Rom. 2:5; cf. 13:12), that Day (2 Thess. 1:10), the Day of the Lord (1 Thess. 5:2; 2 Thess. 2:2; 1 Cor. 5:5), the Day of our Lord Jesus Christ (1 Cor.

1:8), the Day of the Lord Jesus (2 Cor. 1:14), the Day of Christ Jesus (Phil. 1:6), or simply the Day of Christ (Phil. 1:10; 2:16). Paul has adopted and adapted the Day of Yahweh traditions from the Old Testament and applied them to Christ, for now it is Christ who will bring final redemption and judgment to earth. If one compares 1 Thessalonians 4:14-17 and 1 Thessalonians 5:2, it becomes clear that "the Day" is the same as "the Day of the Lord," which in turn is the same as the parousia.

It is in no way surprising that when the phrase "Day of the Lord" is used by Paul, judgment is most frequently spoken of, since it is this phrase that was used most often in the Hebrew Scriptures and Septuagint to speak of coming judgment (cf. Rom. 2:5).[5] Zephaniah 1:15-18; 2:1-3; and 3:8 (cf. Amos 5:18-20; Obad. 15; Joel 1:15; 2:1-2, 31-32; Zech. 14:1-21) stress the idea that the Day of the Lord is a day of God's judgment, though in Obadiah and Zechariah it is also a day of deliverance. Paul says that his audience knows very well (the phrase is emphatic: "you yourselves know very well" [1 Thess. 5:2]) about this matter. There is a note of irony here. The audience knows very well that the timing of the parousia has not been revealed and so is unknown and unpredictable. In addition, Paul says that this day will come like an event at night! If this is not a spectacular use of metaphor and simile, nothing is.

Notice in 1 Thessalonians 5:4-5 we have a clear contrast between believers and unbelievers. Using the darkness and light metaphors, Paul says, in essence, that his converts are not in the state of darkness, nor is the darkness the source of their existence.

They should not be surprised by the coming of the Day of the Lord, even if it arrives at an unexpected time. Believers are children of the day, children of light (cf. Luke 16:8; John 12:36; Eph. 5:8).

Verse 5 is interesting because it calls the audience both sons of light and sons of the day. Here we see the two poles of Paul's eschatology. The light had already dawned in Christ and his converts were already children of light, transformed into new creatures. But they await the day. Provisionally they are also called here "sons of the day," reassuring them they will be participants when Jesus returns.

Notice that Paul says "all" his audience are sons of light and sons of the day. Paul does not hold to a concept of an invisible elect amid the church. He assumes his whole audience believes in Jesus, thus they are among the elect and will be sons of the day. But before they arrive at that day, there is much to prepare for and much to persevere through. They must remember that they are no longer of the night or of darkness.

First Thessalonians 5:9 reassures the converts that God appointed them not to suffer judgment and wrath in the future but rather to receive salvation through "our Lord Jesus Christ." Notice that verse 9 begins with "for." The converts are to put on armor *because* God did not appoint them for wrath. Their destiny is different from that of those referred to as sleeping or drunk in verses 6-7. But of course destinies and destinations can change. Those in darkness may finally see the light, and those in the light may shipwreck their faith. One reason Paul insists on speaking of salvation as something to be obtained in the future is precisely because Christian behavior before one dies or Jesus returns affects the outcome.

Salvation is a gift, whether one is talking about initial or final salvation; but when one is referring to the latter, it is a gift given to those who have persevered, put on the armor, stayed alert, and remained faithful and true. God appoints or destines believers for final salvation (cf. 1 Pet. 2:8). This passage is somewhat like Romans 8:28-29, and in both cases the language of destiny is used to reassure Christians, those who love God, about their future. The subject is not about destining or electing some *to be believers*. Finally, notice that salvation is obtained through the Lord Jesus. He is the medium or agent of salvation, and if one is not connected to him, one cannot obtain final salvation. It is his work on the cross that makes possible the giving of the gift of salvation.

The idea here is that God has provided the believer with the necessary equipment, so that if they will put on the armor, stay awake and alert, and so persevere, they may obtain the gift of final salvation. Paul "does not suggest that God's plan is fulfilled independently of the action of [human beings]. . . . Paul's exhortations to vigilance would be nonsensical if vigilance was the product of some inward causation in the believer by God or if there was no possibility of disobeying the exhortation."[6]

First Thessalonians 4:13-18 and 5:1-11 both conclude with essentially the same final remark. This makes quite clear that Paul is not addressing sequential events in 1 Thessalonians 4:13-18 and 5:1-11. Confirmation that we have been on the right track all along in our interpretation of 1 Thessalonians 4–5 comes when we examine 2 Thessalonians 2, where it is perfectly clear that Christians are to expect only one return of Christ to gather the saints, which comes after the tribulation.

Some think that "parousia" in 1 Thessalonians 4–5 refers to the secret rapture of the church as in 2 Thessalonians 2:1, although they tend to concede that parousia refers to the second coming in this very same argument at 2 Thessalonians 2:8. But Paul everywhere always uses the word *parousia* consistently when speaking of Jesus, referring to the second coming, an all too visible event. The further proof of this comes not only because of the general use of this term to refer to a public event, but also because in this very context in 2 Thessalonians 2:8-9 we note how *parousia* is used in parallel with the verb *revealed* to refer to the public coming of the lawless one. Let us consider 2 Thessalonians 2:1-2 in just a little more detail.

Notice that right off the bat Paul reminds his audience about something of which he has clearly spoken to them before—the parousia and the gathering of the believers to Christ at his coming. These subjects of course were addressed in 1 Thessalonians 5 and 1 Thessalonians 4, respectively. We should compare the use of the term *gathering* to the use of the verbal form of the word in Mark 13:27 and Matthew 24:31, where the verses refer to the gathering together of the believers at the coming of the Son of Man. (Notice the parallel usage in 2 Macc. 2:7,[7] where the verse refers to the "regathering" of Jews into the temporal kingdom after the Babylonian exile.) In 1 Thessalonians 5, Paul is alluding to 1 Thessalonians 4:17 in the use of this term, and so he is speaking of the same event as he spoke of there—the second coming.

What is the upshot of this reading of 1 Thessalonians 4–5, 2 Thessalonians 2, and the other related texts sometimes thought to refer to a rapture? The upshot is that unless by "rapture" one simply means being taken up into the air to welcome Christ and return with him to earth, *there is no theology of the rapture to be found in the New Testament anywhere, never mind the term itself.* But if this is so, what, then, are the implications? Well, if there is no rapture, much of the current popular speculation about the second coming falls down like a house of cards.

For one thing it means that the church of the last generation will go through the fire of tribulation, just as every other generation of Christians has had to do. This is why Jesus' word of comfort in Mark 13:20 is not that we will be spared the tribulation but that God has shortened its time for the sake of the elect people of God, the followers of Jesus. Notice again, for example, what Revelation 12:1-6 in fact promises. The woman, who represents the people of God in this chapter, is not raptured out of the world when the devil pursues her; rather, she is protected from any spiritual harm while remaining in the world. Such is the lot of the people of God in every generation until the Lord returns.

There will be no "beam me up, Scotty" effect for the last generation of Christians. Rather, there will be suffering and martyrdom just as there was in the time when John wrote his Revelation. What was true then will also be true in the end.

Here is where I say that we must be thankful to dispensation-alist people for putting discussion about the end times, and espe-cially the return of Christ, back on the front burner in the last century and a half; and for arguing long, and correctly, that Revelation 20 is, after all, about a millennial reign of Christ on earth. The early church prior to Augustine knew this. The end times just will not involve a pre-tribulation or mid-tribulation rapture. It also will not involve a separate but equal status for eth-nic Israel, now or later.

D. THE MILLENNIUM

In a case of throwing the baby out with the bathwater, some persons have assumed that if there is no doctrine of rapture in the New Testament, then equally there is no concept of a coming millennium before Christ brings in the new heaven and the new earth. This conclusion becomes severely problematic when one actually examines Revelation 19–22 in sequence, a sequence in which John clearly says that a millennium will be followed by a final judgment of Satan and the unbelievers, and this, in turn, will be followed by the new heaven and the new earth. Furthermore, Paul also speaks clearly in 1 Corinthians 15 of a period of time in which Christ must rule on the earth, placing his enemies one by one under his feet, before he finally destroys the last enemy, death, and turns the kingdom back over to the Father. So how did the early church understand such texts and teachings?

The vast majority of early Christian writers who commented on the matter did indeed understand Revelation 20 and texts like 1 Corinthians 15 to refer to a reign of Christ on the earth prior to the end, prior to the final judgment and the new heaven and the new earth.

We may thank figures like Eusebius of Caesarea (ca. 263–339) and Augustine of Hippo (354–430) many centuries after the time of the New Testament writers for changing the way such texts were read. The end result of the change was that in the Middle Ages and thereafter the dominant way of reading a text like Revelation 20 was that it referred to something happening now—during the church age and before the return of Christ. But there are severe problems with such an interpretation.

In the first place, John tells us in Revelation 20:1-4 that during the millennium, Satan will be confined so that he cannot deceive the nations. This, of course, is a direct contradiction of what we hear elsewhere in the New Testament about the role of Satan during church history—namely, that he is a roaring lion capable of deceiving even Christians and destroying others. But there is also a flat contradiction to what Paul says about the first resurrection in 1 Corinthians 15, which dovetails nicely with what John says about the same matter in Revelation 20. Both of these authors distinguish the resurrection of believers from the resurrection of everyone else. What happens when Christ returns is that only believers arise, not everyone. They, then, with a special place given to the martyrs, will reign with Christ upon the earth. As we saw in John 5, Jesus also distinguished between the resurrection of the righteous and the resurrection of those going on to condemnation. Furthermore, there needs to be a time on earth when the things Jesus mentioned would happen at his return actually do so. For example, Jesus speaks of the Twelve sitting on judgment seats in the kingdom, judging the twelve tribes of Israel (Matt. 19:28). This must surely happen before the new heaven and the new earth come to pass. Judgment, of whatever sort, everywhere in the New Testament comes before the very end of all things, before the new heaven and the new earth.

It is thus no surprise that most interpreters in the earliest church believed that a millennial reign on the earth would transpire for a long period of time prior to the final judgment being complete, Satan being destroyed, and the new heaven and the new earth beginning. And this view makes sense of 1 Corinthians 15 as well. Paul says that the last enemy destroyed at the end of the millennial reign will be death. But what does this mean? Death is not a material thing that can have judgment rendered on it.

Surely what Paul is referring to is the same thing John of Patmos refers to as happening at the end of the millennium, namely, the resurrection of everyone else. If there are no dead persons left in the land of the dead, then indeed death has been destroyed once and for all. So, as Revelation 20 says, there is a first resurrection of believers when Christ returns, as Paul indicated in 1 Corinthians 15, and at the millennium's end, there will be a resurrection for those going on to judgment and the lake of fire. Though of course these passages involve some rich and metaphorical imagery, they are nevertheless referential, and the clearest evidence of this fact is the insistence on using the term *resurrection*, which always refers to something that happens to a body. The eschatological scenario now begins to become much clearer:

1. The inauguration of the kingdom of God on earth
2. The death and resurrection of Jesus
3. The destruction of the temple in Jerusalem in A.D. 70
4. The building up of the people of God, the church
5. The proclaiming of the gospel to all nations
6. The second coming/parousia of Christ
7. "All Israel saved" (Rom. 11)
8. The resurrection of the righteous believers and the inheriting of the kingdom
9. The millennium
10. The resurrection of unbelievers and the final judgment on Satan and the lost
11. The new heaven and the new earth

Let us briefly turn to the subject of the new heaven and the new earth. But first we need to stress that God has future plans for both Jew and Gentile united in Jesus the Jewish Messiah. Romans 11 tells us that when Christ returns many Jews will accept him and be saved. So the future is not just about the church, but also about Israel becoming part of "Jew and Gentile united in Christ."

E. THE NEW HEAVEN AND THE NEW EARTH

The end of the Bible speaks volumes about the concerns of our God. God cares about all creation, all creatures great and small. John 3:16 does not mean that God so loved only human beings. It means that he loves the world, both earth and its earthlings, and so he sent his Son to make things right. Jesus understood this particularly clearly when he spoke the promise "The meek shall inherit the earth" (Matt. 5:5). One of my favorite *Far Side* cartoons shows a meek-looking man with a bow tie sitting across the desk from his accountant. The caption below the picture says, "The day after the meek inherit the earth," and the accountant is saying to this meek gentleman, "What you have here, sir, is a pretty serious capital gains problem!" My point is that there needs to be an earth to be inherited when the kingdom comes, and, in any case, earthlings need clean air and water and sun and food to exist at all.

It is no accident that Revelation 22 begins with a vision of a river of life flowing from the throne of God. God is the source of all life, and he wants us to have life and have it abundantly. But again, this requires that we have a place to live and the conditions that are conducive to human life. So the end of the Bible is not just about a new me and a new you, it's about a new heaven and a new earth as well. As that pop icon Sting once asked: "What good would it be to be a new or raised person on an old and poisoned earth?" The vision of redemption in the Bible involves all of creation, just as the beginning of the Bible tells us that God made all things and all creatures and saw that it was good. So it is that the end times in some respects will be like the beginning of all time on earth. The implications of this are profound—God is not merely a creator; he is a conservationist and an ecologist, and earth care should be a part of the agenda of his people as well.

But we need to reflect a bit more in depth on some aspects of Revelation 21–22. In his beautiful poem "Heaven-Haven," Gerard Manley Hopkins puts it this way: "I have desired to go / Where springs not fail / To fields where flies no sharp and sided hail / And a few lilies blow. / And I have asked to be / Where no storms come, / Where the green swell is in the havens dumb, / and out of the swing of the sea."

The Christian journey is not a journey back home, but a journey forward. It has been said that a Jew is a person who faces the past and backs his way into the future, saying, "Tradition, tradition, tradition," but the Christian is a person who looks forward, who "looks homeward, angel," and reminds herself, "The future is as bright as the promises of God." I think that this contrast between Jews and Christians is partially true. But it is striking to me that early Jews of John's day didn't necessarily see life that way. Consider the following quotation from 4 Ezra, a Jewish work written almost at the same time as John's Apocalypse: "For many miseries will affect those who inhabit the world in the last times, because they have walked in great pride. But it is for you that Paradise is opened, the tree of life is planted, the age to come is prepared, plenty is provided, a city is built, rest is appointed, goodness is established, and wisdom is perfected beforehand" (8:48-52). This sounds remarkably like Revelation 21–22.

What is being described in Revelation 21–22 is John of Patmos's dream home, the destiny and destination to which he has been pointed in his vision and to which he points us. John knows that God has put in the heart of every human a home-sickness that can be cured only when one enters the New Jerusalem. Stuck on a godforsaken island, in exile from home and hearth and friends and family, John dreams a big dream of an eternal home, a dream home that was once in heaven, but shall become heaven on earth when Christ returns. It is not a surprise that when John describes this place, this home, this final desti-nation, he thinks of both a beautiful garden like Eden, unspoiled, and a grand city like Jerusalem, untainted by sin and sorrow and suffering, free from disease, decay, and death. He sees our desti-nation not as an escape into a safe haven far away from human-ity like a wildlife sanctuary or a monastery but rather as a pilgrimage into the midst of a city full of people that also contains a garden.

It is as if the monastery and the wildlife sanctuary have been incorporated into the city successfully. In other words, it is as if the harmony between nature and human nature, the peace between human beings and God, has finally been achieved in the presence of the radiant Christ, the bridegroom. But that is not all, for not only does the bridegroom come walking down the stairsteps of heaven to meet the bride, but the heavenly city, the saints, and all that is in it come with him. Heaven comes down and glory will fill our souls. Our ultimate destiny is not, nor has it ever been, to live in a disembodied condition in heaven "forever and ever, amen." Our ultimate destiny is to be fully conformed to the image of Christ by means of resurrection, and thereby made fit to dwell in the New Jerusalem, the Holy City, in which there will be no more sin or suffering or sorrow or disease or decay or death or war or weapons or violence.

Think of it: a hometown with no need of hospitals, no need of police, no need of walls save for ceremonial purposes, no need of firemen or insurance agents, no temple in its midst, for the division between the sacred and the secular will be obliterated forever, all the land will be our Father's land, and all the city will be holy and light, and in it there will be no shadow of turning, no darkness at all, for in him there is no darkness at all. It will be the ultimate family reunion, the ultimate marriage celebration, the ultimate triumph of all that is good and true and beautiful and loving over all that is wicked and false and ugly and hateful. We will not study war anymore; we will not need a Homeland Security division; we will not need politicians to tell us what is best; we will not need to be pointed toward God, for we will be dwelling right in his midst—Immanuel. Faith will become sight, hope will be realized, and perfect love will cast out all fear. John is saying to us, "Don't sell your ticket to the final destination for the lesser good of dying and going to be with Jesus."

We enter this final destination by finally being fully conformed to the image of Christ by means of a resurrection. Then, indeed, we may talk in the full sense of Christian perfection, nothing less than the full conformity to the image of Christ in body as well as in mind and spirit and emotions.

This home is not achieved; it is to be received. It is not accomplished; it is entered by grace through faith. It is a city in which God himself condescends and there is a corporate merger between heaven and earth, and God will personally wipe away every tear from every eye. The future is so bright we will all need shades, as we are told there will be no more night. The future is so bright that in this city we will not only have all we need, we will have all we want and want only all we have. The future is so bright that there will even be the healing of the memories as is symbolized by the medicinal trees meant for healing in the golden city. And we will reign forever and ever on earth with our God and with his Christ. Talk about an extreme home makeover!

Some years ago I was called upon to do the funeral service for my grandfather in Wilmington, North Carolina. He had lived a long, rich life into his nineties and had been a devout Christian and member of his Baptist church. The time came for the interment service at the old graveyard, and the funeral directors were about to crank my grandfather down into the ground, when an impulse struck me. I had not seen Pop, as I had arrived after the visiting hours and the casket had been closed throughout the service in the church and at the graveyard. I asked them to open the casket for a moment, and I went over and kissed my grandfather on the forehead and said, "Good-bye, Pop," but then I thought—*No.* He is not gone; he has just gone on to the heavenly resting station, an interim stop on the way to the new heaven and the new earth. And so instead I would now say, having learned from John, "I'll see you at home."

Our final destiny, privilege, and task are indeed to adore and love God and enjoy him forever, casting down our golden crowns before the glassy sea. With the whole company of heaven, with all the saints of the past, and now we will experience exultation, adoration, celebration, jubilation, coronation, and destination all wrapped into one. All that is good and true and beautiful will finally triumph over all that is dark and dangerous and dastardly. Home is not merely where the heart longs to be, home is our future permanent dwelling place where God, who is eternal life, lives in our midst and, therefore, there is no place for disease, decay, death, suffering, sin, or sorrow. There could be no more dramatic or satisfying climax to the Bible than what we find in Revelation 21–22.

That this material uses broadly understood metaphorical symbols and is not literally descriptive should not lead us to assume that it is not referring to something real that John believed existed. John's primary focus, like that of most biblical writers, is on the redemption and judgments of God in space and time. As such, he shares an essential kinship with other prophets and seers in the Jewish and Christian tradition who are concerned about the future of God's people not merely in heaven but on earth. This is one thing that distinguishes John from those who simply have mystical visions of heaven or who go on otherworldly tours. While it could be argued that John had an otherworldly tour in the Spirit, it appears more likely that John's experience was simply a matter of receiving certain revelations one after another. His account does not read like Enoch's tour of heaven.

It cannot be stressed enough that one of the functions of a work like Revelation is to give early Christians perspective, especially in regard to the matters of good and evil, redemption and judgment. Revelation seeks to peel back the veil and reveal to the audience the underlying supernatural forces at work behind the scenes that are affecting what is going on at the human level. A certain limited dualism is evident in this literature. The message is often this: though it appears that evil is triumphing, God is still in his heaven and all in due course will be right with the world. Biblical books like Revelation stress that the goal of life is ultimately beyond death in either the afterlife or the afterworld on earth or both. There is also usually a strong sense of alienation and powerlessness, and thus a major stress on God's sovereignty and divine intervention in human affairs, especially on transcendent solutions to human dilemmas, though human efforts are not rendered meaningless.

F. MULTIVALENT SYMBOLS

Here is a good place to say a bit more about the use of multivalent symbols in Revelation. It is true that the wounded beast in Revelation 13 and 17 probably does allude to Nero; but with the help of mythological imagery, Nero is portrayed as but a representative example of a higher supernatural evil—the antichrist figure. The author knows that Nero does not exhaust the meaning of the figure, but he certainly exemplifies it well. There could be other such figures as well, for the author is dealing with types. These symbols are plastic, flexible, and on the order of character analysis rather than literal description. Christ is depicted in Revelation as the blood-drenched warrior or a lamb who was slain, or a lion, or an old man with snow-white hair. All these descriptions are meant to reveal some aspect of his character and activity. In this respect, these symbols are much like some modern political cartoons.

Apocalyptic literature is basically minority literature and often even sectarian literature, the product of a subset of a subculture in the Greco-Roman world. While it is not always true that such literature was written in a time of crisis or for a people currently experiencing persecution, it is certainly written for people who feel vulnerable in a world that largely does not concur with their own worldview. In the case of Revelation, there is probably enough internal evidence to suggest that there had been some persecution and even martyrdom with more expected.

It is not surprising, then, that apocalyptic prophecy often has a political dimension, dealing with the dominant human powers that appear to be shaping the destiny of God's people. Whether it is Revelation portraying Rome as a modern-day Babylon or Daniel portraying a succession of beastly empires, there is frequent discussion of these matters, but one must understand the referents and sense the drift of the polemic and promises. This aspect of apocalyptic literature grows directly out of the classical

Jewish prophetic material where nations and rulers, including Israel's, are critiqued, but here this is carried out by "outsiders" (those who do not have controlling access to the political process) using insiders' language.

There is such a strong stress on God's control over the final human ultimate destiny in literature about the end times that when in fact one gets to the final showdown, it turns out to be not a battle between human forces, which we might call Armageddon, but rather a divine execution. Consider, for example, 2 Thessalonians 2:8. At verse 8 we arrive at the same juncture in time as in 2 Thessalonians 2:3, with verses 6-7 dealing with the prelude to the final acts in the end-time scenario. It is not made clear how long the lawless one will operate unhindered before Christ returns. The issue is to reveal his ultimate downfall. One of the most interesting features of this verse is that it makes clear that the final judgment of the lawless one will be accomplished by word rather than by war; indeed, by the breath of Jesus' mouth. Compare how in Revelation 19:21 the rider on the white horse (aka Christ) executes the kings of the earth and their armies by the sword of the word coming out of Messiah's mouth. We may compare how in Revelation 20:7-10 the final judgment of Gog and Magog transpires also by direct divine action, in this case fire from heaven. There will be no final great battle between human forces called Armageddon, only a final divine execution as is described in various ways in these texts. This makes all speculation about some great Middle Eastern war between human combatants not only wasted, but odious; since in fact the New

Testament suggests a different endgame scenario involving direct divine intervention.

G. THE GEMATRIA GAME AND HOW NUMBERS COUNT

There is certainly a great fascination in apocalyptic literature with symbolic numbers, and so something more must be said about gematria. Gematria is a system of assigning numerical value to a word or phrase in the belief that the words or phrases with identical numerical values have a special relation to one another.

In the Bible there are, of course, some oft-repeated numbers: 3, 4, 7, 10, 12, and their multiples. Knowing that seven denotes completion or perfection helps in understanding not only why there are the number of seals that there are in Revelation (a complete and comprehensive set of judgments), but also why the antichrist figure is numbered 666, which signifies chaos and incompletion. There is also a tendency in this literature to speak of time elusively or elliptically—such as Daniel's "a time, a time and a half, and a time," or his famous interpretation of Jeremiah's seventy weeks (Dan. 12:7). Yet, it is surprisingly rare to find in either Jewish or Christian apocalypses any sort of precise calculations about how many days or years are left before the end.

Scholars have often puzzled over the different numbers, apparently referring to the same time period in Daniel 12:11-12, but it need not be a case of recalculation or later editorial change. If the numbers are symbolic in nature (for example, multiples of seven, or one half of seven), they should probably not be taken as attempts, much less failed attempts, at precise calculation. What such numbers do suggest when they describe periods of time is that matters are determined or fixed already by God, and thus God is still in control so that evil and suffering will at some point in time cease. The message of such numbers is: "this too will pass," or "this too will come to pass." They were not meant to encourage ancient or modern forecasting.

But what if justice is deferred or not seen to be done in a reasonable period of time? Certainly one of the major reasons for apocalyptic literature is this sense of justice deferred or denied for the minority group, which leads to a robust emphasis on vindication not only in the afterlife, but more important, in the end times. It is not an accident that apocalypses often manifest interest in justice and political issues on the one hand and the other-world and the afterlife on the other. There is a relationship between these two things: if there is no life to come, then many of the wrongs done in this life will never be rectified, and God's justice will be called into question.

Apocalyptic literature, and especially prophecy about the end times, is often an attempt to deal with the issue of theodicy, by which I mean the problem of why God's people suffer and why there is evil if there is also a good, all-powerful God. For instance, Revelation reassures the saints about not only individual vindication in the afterlife, but also justice for God's people in the end. Indeed, it is at the point where cosmology and history meet, when heaven comes down to earth in the form of the Messiah and the New Jerusalem, that there is finally both resolution and reward for the saints and a solution to the human dilemma caused by suffering and evil. Suffering and death are overcome by resurrection and everlasting life, and evil is overcome by the Last Judgment. Obviously, the persuasiveness of this depends entirely on the audience's belief in not only a transcendent world but also a God who actually cares enough to intervene in human history and set things right once and for all.

But the very fact that this sort of information is conveyed only through visions, dreams, and oracles makes clear that, without revelation, without the unveiling of divine secrets and mysteries, humans would be in the dark about such matters. The message of apocalyptic literature is that the meaning and purpose of human history cannot finally be discovered simply by empirical study or analysis. This does not mean that the author has given up on history, as is sometimes asserted, but rather that he is placing his trust not in what humans can accomplish in history, but in what God can finally make of history.

H. AND SO?

What is the upshot of this discussion?

1. To take apocalyptic prophecy literally is to *violate* the character of such prophecy, which, while referential, uses metaphors and images.

2. To strip either regular oracles or apocalyptic prophecies out

of their historical context and to fail to realize that much of this material has already been fulfilled in generations gone by is a major mistake.

3. Even when one is dealing with prophetic material in Revelation that focuses on events that are still outstanding, such as the second coming of Christ, it is critical to bear in mind that Old Testament and New Testament writers were not writing with us in mind. We must enter their world. They are not speaking directly in our language.

4. Careful study will show that even in Revelation judgment is not ever exercised by anyone other than divine agents—Jesus or his angels or those who come with him from heaven. There will be no Armageddon between human armies. There will be no rebuilding of the temple in Jerusalem by human forces—all divine solutions to the human dilemma descend from above. They do not have to do with human machinations, invasions, and plans. Neither America nor any other nation is depicted as dealing with the antichrist. Only the rider on the white horse can do that. One should not look to the modern secular State of Israel as some sort of fulfillment of biblical Israel. Not even orthodox Jews in Israel see the current government in Israel as biblical!

5. At no point in biblical prophecy, either Jewish or Christian, are there envisioned two separate peoples of God to whom differing groups of prophecy apply. Always the people of God are either Jews with Gentile adherents united in Israel or, in the later Christian schema, Jew and Gentile united in Christ.

6. From a Christian point of view, all Old Testament promises and prophecies are to be fulfilled in or by Christ, not apart from Christ and/or the church.

7. It is true that some of this biblical prophecy is predictive, and some of it is eschatological in character and has not yet come to pass. It is often, however, not as particularistic in character as some interpreters might like. Perhaps this is because God reveals enough of the future to give us hope, but not so much that we no longer need to exercise faith!

In this brief study, we have barely skimmed the surface of many interesting topics involving the end times. There is so much more that could and should be said, which is why at the outset we recommended a book like *Jesus, Paul and the End of the World*, or *The Problem with Evangelical Theology*, if you are interested in further study. What I have attempted to do in this little book is tease your mind into active thought about what the Bible says regarding our future, and help you get oriented when thinking about this series of interrelated and fascinating, but sometimes bewildering, topics. The Bible affirms that in the end God's will shall be done on earth as it is in heaven, and the kingdoms of this world will become the kingdom of our Lord, and all manner of things will be well as the saints go marching into the new heaven and the new earth. It is a consummation devoutly to be wished, and the good part is, it is not merely a dream or a wish, it's the plan of an almighty God for us, and as the Bible says, "God is faithful, and he will do it."

NOTES

1. THE CHARACTER OF BIBLICAL PROPHECY

1. See Witherington, *Jesus the Seer: The Progress of Prophecy* (Peabody, Mass.: Hendrickson, 2000). The material in the next few pages of this book appears in a much more complete and complicated form there.

2. J. J. Collins, ed., *Apocalypse: The Morphology of a Genre, Semeia* 14 (1979), p. 9. To this definition, D. Helholm added the suggestion that it is literature intended for a group in crisis with the intent of exhortation or consolation by means of divine authority.

3. One can begin to recognize the sea change in eschatology when one compares and contrasts Revelation with the Shepherd of Hermas. See my *Jesus the Seer,* pp. 371–78.

2. THE RETURN OF THE KING

1. Josephus was the famous first-century A.D. Jewish historian.

2. Ernest Best, *The First and Second Epistles to the Thessalonians* (New York: Continuum, 1986), p. 354.

3. THE OTHER WORLD—HEAVEN AND HELL

1. Don Piper with Cecil Murphey, *90 Minutes in Heaven: A True Story of Death and Life* (Grand Rapids: Revell, 2004).

4. RAISING THE DEAD

1. See N. T. Wright, *The Resurrection of the Son of God* (Minneapolis: Fortress Press, 2003).

2. One might well ask, *But why, then, did Jesus retain wound marks or scars?* The point is that there is continuity between Jesus' old body and his new one. It is the old body that has been raised and transformed by God's resurrection power.

5. THE AFTERLIFE

1. This material appears in another and longer, more technical form in my *The Problem with Evangelical Theology* (Waco, Tex.: Baylor University Press, 2005).

2. J. M. Canfield, *The Incredible Scofield*, 2nd edition (Vallecito, Calif.: Ross House Books, 2005).

3. It is not possible to deal with all the enormous exegetical and theological problems that dispensationalism presents us with, and so the reader is directed to the study by B. Rossing, *The Rapture Exposed: The Message of Hope in the Book of Revelation* (Boulder, Colo.: Westview, 2004), and to the fine and more general study of eschatology by C. Hill, *In God's Time: The Bible and the Future* (Grand Rapids: Eerdmans, 2002), see especially pp. 199–209 on the rapture. One point that should be stressed is that, as Hill points out, the dispensationalist system is an ever-evolving thing, and now we even have "progressive" dispensationalism (see C. A. Blaising and D. L. Bock, *Progressive Dispensationalism* [Wheaton: Bridgepoint, 1993]), which rejects the original idea of Darby that the Christian era was a mere parenthesis in between the two parts of the story of Israel, involving prophecy and its fulfillment. This theory suggests that the rapture gets the church off the earthly scene so the rest of the Old Testament prophecies can come true literally for Israel. The problem of course with this is that various New Testament authors think these same prophecies are being fulfilled by Christ and in the new people of God, which are Jew and Gentile united in Christ. This theory of Darby's is especially ironic since Paul sees the Mosaic era and its legislation and prophecies as the parenthesis in between the Abrahamic and new covenants, the latter being the fulfillment of the former, and the promises to Abraham coming to fruition in Jesus.

4. We may point out that Paul is capable of talking about events that must precede the parousia, as a way of making clear that the end is not yet at hand, but he does not speak of these events as sign markers or events that trigger the return of Christ and so must be closely juxtaposed in time with the parousia.

5. The Septuagint is the Greek translation of the Old Testament used by Paul and others in that era.

6. I. H. Marshall, *1 and 2 Thessalonians* (Vancouver: Regent College Publishing, 2002), pp. 139–40.

7. First and Second Maccabees are Jewish books written before the time of Jesus about the Jewish battles to retake the Holy Land from its oppressors.

Printed in the USA
CPSIA information can be obtained
at www.ICGtesting.com
LVHW080243130224
771596LV00039B/961